VISIBILITY ONLINE

6 STEPS TO SUCCESS – BUILDING A STRONG DIGITAL BUSINESS

Business ideas that really makes money.
Build a WordPress website.
#1 in Google with SEO.
Effective advertising.
Usability.
Web analytics.

BERNAT RIERA

ISBN-13: 978-84-697-6141-0

http://bernatriera.es/en/

DEDICATION

To those who don't settle and are seeking continuous improvement.
To those who are keen to learn and to be entrepreneurs.

To my mother—the only one who always pushed me to do it, no matter what. To my wife—who watches me patiently while I'm doing it.

CONTENT

WHAT WILL HAPPEN FOR YOU BY THE END OF THIS BOOK? 9

STEP 1: MAKE MONEY WHILE YOU SLEEP 11
1. GENERATE MORE INCOME PER HOUR 13
2. WEBSITE AS AN EXTENSION OF YOUR PHYSICAL BUSINESS OR AS A BUSINESS IN ITSELF 15
3. IDEAS TO CREATE A POTENTIAL ONLINE BUSINESS 18
4. CREATING YOUR NEW BRAND 25
5. UNDERSTANDING YOUR USERS AND CUSTOMERS 27
6. HOW A WEBSITE CAN GENERATE INCOME 31
7. CREATING A SUCCESSFUL ONLINE STORE 38
8. SELL YOUR PRODUCTS ON AMAZON 41

STEP 2: WEB DEVELOPMENT AND ECOMMERCE 45
9. BUYING YOUR HOSTING AND DOMAIN 47
10. WEB DEVELOPMENT WITH WORDPRESS 56
11. WEB DESIGN THROUGH TEMPLATES AND PLUGINS 65
12. SECURITY ON YOUR WORDPRESS 77
13. FAST LANE: LANDING PAGE DEVELOPMENT 80
14. CREATE A LANDING PAGE IN 25 MIN WITH INSTAPAGE 84
15. SHOPIFY AS AN ALTERNATIVE ECOMMERCE 89

STEP 3: SEO - SEARCH ENGINE OPTIMIZATION ON GOOGLE 93
16. SEO: FREE VISIBILITY ON GOOGLE 95
17. SEO TECHNIQUES FOR YOUR WEBSITE 100
18. EXTRA SEO TRICKS FOR ECOMMERCE 128
19. UPDATING YOUR SITE WITHOUT IMPACTING ITS SEO 130
20. TOOLS TO AUDIT THE SEO OF A WEBSITE 132
21. THE NEAR FUTURE OF SEO 137

STEP 4: ONLINE ADVERTISING 141
22. GET RESULTS TODAY WITH ONLINE ADVERTISING 143
23. ADS IN GOOGLE SEARCH 147
24. ADS IN GOOGLE DISPLAY NETWORK (GDN) 172
25. ADS IN GMAIL 180
26. ADS IN YOUTUBE 182
27. ADS IN GOOGLE SHOPPING ADS - PLA'S 185
28. ADS IN FACEBOOK & INSTAGRAM 188
29. ADS IN TWITTER 195
30. ADS IN LINKEDIN 198
31. RETARGET YOUR PREVIOUS VISITS 201

STEP 5: USABILITY AND USER EXPERIENCE 207
32. WHAT ARE USABILITY AND USER EXPERIENCE? 209
33. FEATURES OF A GOOD WEB EXPERIENCE 211
34. HOME PAGE DESIGN 216
35. USABILITY FOR ONLINE STORES 219
36. TOOLS TO IMPROVE AND ANALYSE USABILITY 224

STEP 6: ANALYSIS AND MEASUREMENT 235
37. GOOGLE ANALYTICS: ANALYSIS OF YOUR WEB TRAFFIC 237
38. GOOGLE SEARCH CONSOLE 252
39. GOOGLE ADSENSE: MONETISATION REPORT 257
40. GOOGLE DATA STUDIO: REPORT OF REPORTS 259
41. SUPERMETRICS FOR MULTIPLE DATA SOURCES 261
42. HOOTSUITE FOR YOUR SOCIAL NETWORKS 264

WHAT WILL HAPPEN FOR YOU BY THE END OF THIS BOOK?

I want you to get your business booming as soon as possible, so I'll keep this introduction brief.

I'm not here to fill excess pages, but to boil the vital information down as efficiently as possible so that it is quick and easy to read. By the end of this book you should be able to create a web page, position it in Google, and get the maximum performance for your business, whether online or physical.

You will not need to know code or graphic design, and you will save a fortune on web developers, designers, and online marketing companies. You will be ahead of the competition in search engines, which is where all your users and customers start their purchase journey.

I want you to be able to go from scratch to having a beautiful website for your business, rank in top positions on Google, launch advertising campaigns in different media channels with the confidence of reaching your potential customers at the lowest cost, and help you with ideas on how to monetise web pages.

For entrepreneurs and small-to-medium business owners.

At the end of this book, you will be generating customers and income while playing with your children, while fishing, or playing football. While developing your next business. As you sleep.

STEP 1

MAKE MONEY WHILE YOU SLEEP

1. GENERATE MORE INCOME PER HOUR

Perhaps, you started reading this book with a clear idea about the website you wanted to develop, maybe to get more online visibility for your business or to carry out a new business idea that you wished to try without spending a fortune in the experiment.

I hope that by the time you get to the end of this book, a sea of new opportunities and ideas for new websites will have opened up for you, besides covering the ones you already had in mind; and that you can create them without much effort, leading you to creating a unique website that will serve as a sustainable online business.

Before developing a website, it's important you're clear about functionality and the goal of your page. This is the fastest and most direct route towards success. Also, have a constant online presence. Having one gives immense profitability.

Remember: you'll never get rich if you exchange your time for a salary, since your time is limited. Your only goal every year should be that every hour of work daily must always generate more and more income for you:

$$Your\ income\ per\ hour = \frac{Total\ income\ from\ any\ source}{Total\ hours\ worked\ in\ all\ your\ money\ sources}$$

Where the total income is summed up from your office salary, the rent of your tenants if you have any, the income of your web pages, etc., while the total hours worked would be the ones dedicated to generate that income: hours at the office, hours managing your rented apartments, developing web pages, etc.

A day has 24hours, but nature demands we sleep for about 8hours. This leaves us with only 16hours left to generate income, to eat, rest, take a shower, and spend time with our families. Wait, go back! Let me shock with this: we should even be generating money during the 8hours we sleep!

There are two formulas that work very well to make money while you sleep:

1. Buy a property.
2. Have an online business which is opened for 24hours.

Presently, I'll explain the second one. However, for the first formula, I strongly recommend reading some other books about property investment.

2. WEBSITE AS AN EXTENSION OF YOUR PHYSICAL BUSINESS OR AS A BUSINESS IN ITSELF

A WEB TO PROMOTE YOUR PHYSICAL BUSINESS

If you want to create a web page to generate an extension and an online presence of your physical space: like your store, gym or office, the rewards of your efforts invested in learning to create a website plus the investment you put on online advertising are already totally justified. Your income source is clear: engage more and new clients from your location.

Your users are at home (or anywhere) and they suddenly have a need: some want to buy a product; others are looking for the closest gym or finding a new administrator for their tax refund. To satisfy these needs, they browse on their computers or mobiles and you just make sure you are there; in those Google search results, as high as possible, and most importantly, on top of your competitors.

Throughout the book, I'll show you how to always have a competitive edge in the world called Google and be present for any relevant search in your line of business, besides learning how to launch advertising campaigns in the channels where the users in your city are.

If your real business is a store, you'll discover how to extend it digitally and take your products to all their homes with no need for your potential clients to walk by your window store. The only aspects you'll have to define are the inventory and their deliveries. I'll explain the best practices of the most successful ecommerce webs and which platform you'll be able to create them in an easy and very professional way.

If you're ready to get started, then go directly to the second step. However, if you read these chapters completely, you can develop different points of view from the ones you have now. Perhaps you'll find out that you could add a new service to increase your profitability. Maybe at the end, you'll make your business evolve more than expected due the digital ideas you will learn from these chapters. And if I'm honest with you, that's a very good sign. You will probably have a more prosperous future than those businessmen that think their clients aren't on Instagram. Come, follow me steadily.

A WEB TO PROMOTE YOUR ONLINE BUSINESS

I will stimulate your brain to the point you will hit the spot that will make you execute your idea. But be patient. You know light bulbs don't usually turn on when one wants them to. You'll have to be observant and identify opportunities in your activities. Think about how everything you do could be improved upon, even if just a little, and be made more efficient, faster, cheaper or easier. Either you create a web page offering something that doesn't exist or improve on something that's already there.

A big first step is to pause for at least 20 seconds every time you make a search on Google and open your eyes and senses to see if there's an online opportunity. Observe the results, but don't add extra keywords to redefine your search, since the rest of the users probably searched just like you did and also didn't find what they were looking for. Wouldn't it be interesting to create an optimised website for these keywords and get that space on Google?

Good stuff. Write that down and keep analysing: click on the first 5 results that appear and open them in different tabs. Now yes, refine your initial search by adding more keywords and click again on the new 5 results. Once all the tabs are open, visit them one by one and analyse these:

- Are these websites good enough to cover your needs?
- Don't condition yourself browsing through them like the webmaster suggested with the navigation menu. Instead, try to

discover what you'd want to do in them and check if that's available or possible.

- Did you end in very generic pages or directories like Yellow pages, Gumtree or eBay, that cover too much and you would've preferred to get something much more specific?

With these searches and analyses of the results, you might have already detected the opportunity I was referring to. If Google didn't find anything better to show you, it's because no one has created it or optimised it. If the existing webs haven't given you a good experience, then perhaps it's time for someone to improve them and offer a better one to the users. And if finally, you ended up in much more generic pages than you expected, like directories, perhaps you've detected a niche market with a huge opportunity. Perhaps you think you wouldn't have the sufficient number of specific visits, however, believe me, there are many people out there that is searching for it like you just did.

If you're still not getting anything good, bring some more papers and pen to this book because we'll keep brainstorming on it together in subsequent chapters.

3. IDEAS TO CREATE A POTENTIAL ONLINE BUSINESS

DETECT OPPORTUNITIES IN THE MARKET

The best way to find an idea for a good money making online business is by detecting one of the following opportunities:

- Solving a problem about something you've experienced, like you noticed in the previous exercise.
- A lack in a concrete industry.
- A new technology, app or software that can be used in another way or in another country.

When you start to think about an idea, find out who your potential customers are. If your answer is that everyone can be your customer, then it means you don't have the business idea yet. You need to find a niche market, and the more specific you are, the better.

Besides, the more unique and concrete the niche is, the easier it will be to have a good online ranking and become a reference. On the flip side, if you want to cover too much or position yourself as something very generic, it will cost you more to become the leader online. An extreme example would be to create an online store only for blue shoe laces *versus* a clothing store that includes t-shirts, dresses, shoes and also blue shoe laces. Which one do you think would dominate the market quicker and easier? The former of course!

INVESTIGATE AND ANALYSE YOUR CHANCES OF SUCCESS

It's a very important step to determine the possibilities of success of your business idea. Don't skip this step and make sure you know the answers to these questions:

- What's the size of my market/industry?
- What competitors are online?
- What's the industry's dynamic, its growth, its online penetration, and the experience from mobile or other devices?
- What is, what was and what will be its price? Of what economic units are we talking about? 10's€, 100's€ or 1.000's€?

There are three ways to discover all of this information:

1. Pay a third party to research it for you. Use the information that another company has already paid for:
2. Find public companies from the same sector and industry that are in the stock market such as a competitor, a manufacturer of the product or a supplier of the service.

   Look for the investor-section in their website and download PDFs related to sales, profits and what interests us: this 'market research', which will give us real data about the overall industry and its trends.
3. Do some research online with the tools I'll talk about next.

Ask Google its opinion using their online and public tools:

Google Ad Preview Tool

This tool will help you to simulate and visualise the real Google search results in any location in the world, in any language, using any Google domain (.es, .com, .co.uk, etc.) and from any device (mobile, tablets or computers). These are the four simple parameters you will have to configure when you access the link: https://adwords.google.com/apt/AdPreview.

According to the parameters you set in the visualization, Google will provide you with some results or others, since its algorithm takes into account all these. That means, it doesn't show the same results to a user in London than on in Manchester or New York, even though both of them searched in English on Google.com.

I like to use this tool as a true display of my competition for a particular user. If my clients try to look for my business when they're on the move (and I own a petrol station), then it's essential that the results appear on a mobile device and provide a good mobile experience.

If I own a travel agency and my users visit it online from all around the world, I will have to see who I compete against in specific locations like Colombia when they look for flights, hotels or transportation for Seville (Spain).

The following screenshot shows a preview of the results after the search 'running shoes' made from a laptop in London on Google.co.uk and with a browser in English language.

The results show me a list of advertisers showing paid results in several formats, like a list of products for sale on the top and normal ads, which shows it's a very competitive term, so I know that if I want to reach those customers, I'll have to compete online with MandMDirect and SportsDirect among others.

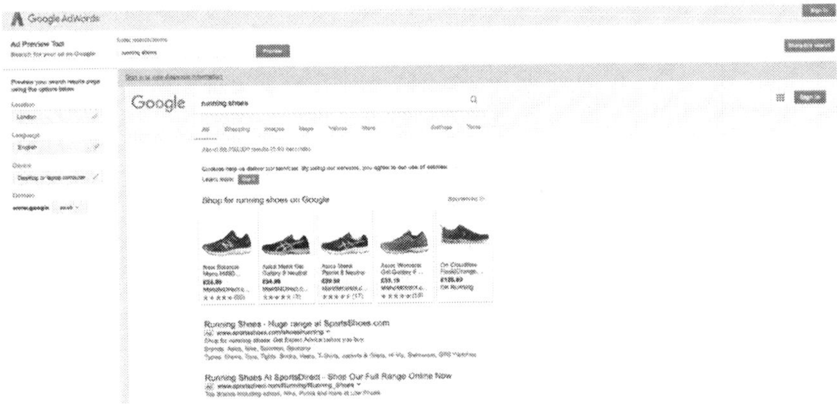

Google Trends

Google provides a history of searches for any word or phrase, filterable both by country as well as date and within a specific category: https://www.google.es/trends/.

Besides providing the trends of the search volume for those words during a period of time, Google Trends also allows you to compare alternative phrases. This makes it very useful when you are in doubt about which set of words you'll have to optimise in your web. That means, if you have an online store of shoes for different sports, through Google Trends, you'd understand that if you want to attract a larger number of visits, your optimization should be more around 'football boots' rather than 'sports shoes', since even though the latter is more generic and you think you could capture more traffic, people define their searches more specifically.

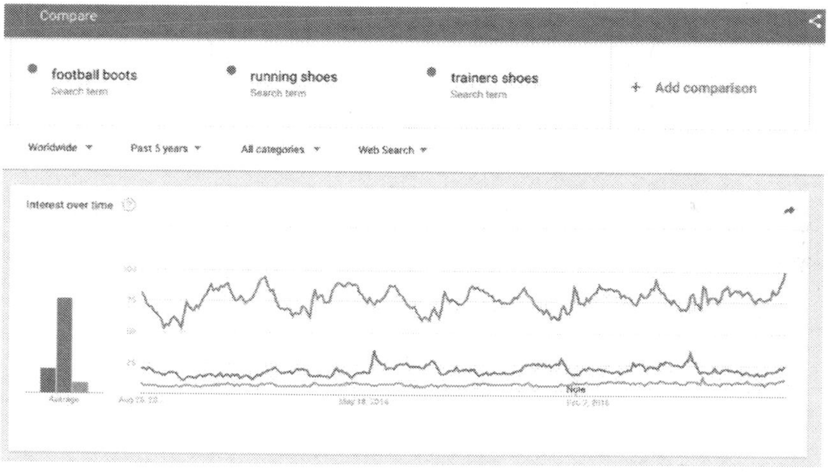

Google Keyword Planner

Google's keyword planner exists in reality to support those who create advertising campaigns in the search engine and need to expand their combination of keywords to have more complete campaigns and reach more users.

Additionally, it advices about how you can group these words into different sets: it states the volume of searches, the potential traffic these words will get (clicks) and how much you should bid on keywords in case of doing an advertising campaign in AdWords, which is an indicator of the competition and advertisers that are already bidding to appear in the results.

Advertising campaigns in Google, and in most of the online channels, are based on a bidding system: the more you pay, the more visibility you get. However, you'll be able to learn all of this in more details in the online advertising step.

To use this tool, you'll have to create a Google AdWords account that you can easily set up for free with any Gmail address.

Just access: https://adwords.google.com/KeywordPlanner and follow the steps on the screen without entering any payment system, since you only want to use it to analyse the market for this exercise.

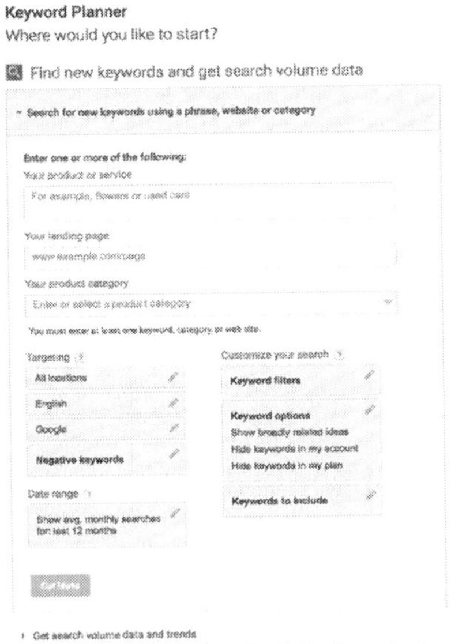

You'll see that 4 different analysis options will be presented, but to analyse our business idea, its chances of success and how the competition is doing, you simply need to use 'Search for new keywords using a phrase, website or category'.

Enter new keywords into the first box related to your product or service. This will extend the list and show you the volume of searches as it's displayed in the following image, in which I entered 'sports shoes, football boots, running shoes'.

Google shows us a chart with the search volumes for those keywords from month to month, indicating that summer and December are the peaks where people search more for related terms.

On the other hand, in the tab 'Keyword ideas', you'll get an expanded list about which related terms are more searched for. This will help you to define your idea about creating or optimizing your new website focused in some words more than others.

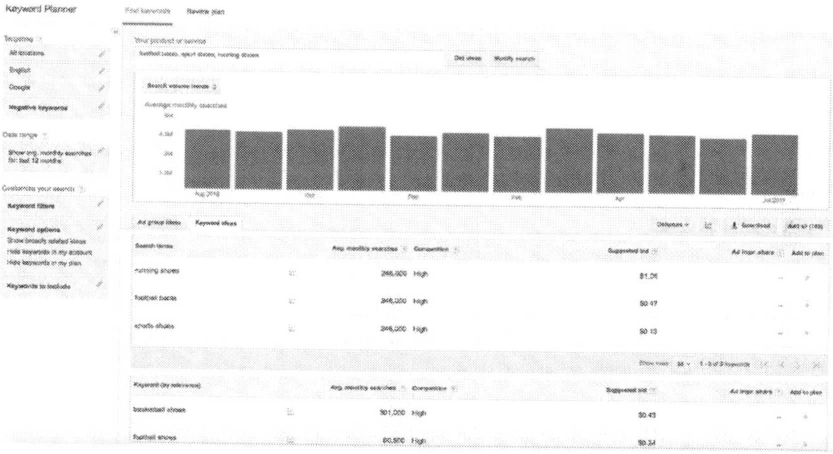

Additionally, you can also look for a list of words entering a URL, possibly one of our potential competitors we observed in the 'Ad preview tool' (http://www.sportsdirect.com/the-boot-room) since with it, we'll get the list of the most used words in that page and their search volume, with which you can get a slight idea about the times that the web is suggested to its users by Google.

4. CREATING YOUR NEW BRAND

Lose the fear to fail

If everything points to an opportunity for success and you're motivated to start, that's great! The good thing about creating an online business is that you can begin without taking a lot of risk or having to invest a large amount in advance.

But I have a few more questions before you definitely go for it:

- Are you ready to fail? Know that the first version of your website or even your business idea in general can fail. At least that's the worst case scenario, although everything you've learnt in the process can still be reinvested in your next idea. But if failing is a nightmare for you, then you better don't get started.
- Do I do it alone or want a co-founder? It's good to gather different skills in a team. A team member could be very good at sales and another in app development. Or both of them in marketing, to set an example. The essential thing to keep in mind is that both members should be able to add value to the business. This should be clearly defined from the beginning so as to avoid bringing in someone that subtracts more than they add to the business.
- Do I have the capital for the first acquisition of users / products?
- Everything will happen very fast if you accelerate it properly. Here you should invest 80% of your budget, since there won't be another thing that more clearly defines the potential of your business.

Years may pass by before your page has significant traffic to monetise it or till it gets an interesting number of users. So if your app makes sense and you don't want to wait for long, you should have a good amount of money to invest in online advertising and acquire new customers. Once you get this, your business will roll like a snowball, but the hardest part is always the beginning.

Develop the brand: think long term

Before starting anything at all, define your brand well and invest in it. It's something that won't show immediate results, but it will mark your reputation throughout time.

Define which will be your tone when talking on your website, on your blog and in your customer service. Define the colours that will come along throughout your web, your cards, your presentations.

And above all, define the company's principles: why does it exist? what values does it have? and which is the mission?

5. UNDERSTANDING YOUR USERS AND CUSTOMERS

ANALYSIS OF YOUR 'PERSONAS' OR VISITORS

Although this is a very important step in designing a webpage, it's usually forgotten by the main decision makers, like the CMOs or CEOs of small and medium sized companies.

In an interview with them, acting as a digital marketing consultant, I asked: 1) how does your company earn money through the web? and 2) who are the 'personas' who will give you that money?

Even though many doubt the first question, very few had any idea about the second one. At most, they were only able to answer if the target audience were customers (B2C) or companies (B2B).

The analysis of personas helps in defining certain key users of your web who will be the potential customers generating revenue. If you don't know who they are, how they search, act, or pay, how will you design an optimised webpage for them? At best, you're optimizing it for yourself.

So for instance, if you have an art marketplace, your 'personas' are two: artists who create and sell art and art buyers. Your online business won't exist if one of them is missing.

If you don't have sellers on your website, you won't have products, visits or buyers. If you don't have buyers, the sellers will disappear with time or they simply won't discover your website in the first place.

Here is another less commercial example; Let's say you have a dance academy, your *three personas* are:

- The *students* that want to sign up, so the page should inform them about the classes, prices and schedules. You must have a presence on Google so when they are interested, they can find you, but also a very good presence on social media sites like Facebook to refine your target in persuading new apprentices. For example, perhaps your campaign is more focused on finding boys/men that want to dance, since the demand could be lower. The students are the ones that make money for your business.

- On the other hand, the *dance teachers*, who will play an important part in the development and motivation of the students. The teachers will be a cost for your business, but if you don't have them or you hire bad ones, it will have a negative impact in the registration and progress of students.
- To catch online the interest of the teachers who may be employed by other academies, you should find them using advertisements on the relevant websites they usually visit, websites dedicated to dance teachers, competitions, dance videos in YouTube, etc. So the Display and YouTube advertising could be your key of success.
- And once they go to your website, don't forget them. Create contents for them such as specific content, images, videos and information about the academy's reputation for them.
- And as an additional third persona, we have the *dance competition organizations.* You want them to see you as a clear representative of your city to go to contests and awards, therefore your page should be cared for and updated constantly, showing a lot of reviews by students, teachers and professionals. Be on top in in Google so it can be interpreted that you're the best academy and not only because you know how to optimise your web.
- To influence those organizations, it will be important to have presence in LinkedIn and connect with their employees and keep posting relevant content.

Each *persona* in your business has to be clearly identified and approach with the best creative in the right channel.

You can start to create 'personas' in your business by creating an individual card with a fake name, an image and certain points of relevant information like:

- Name
- Company and position
- Hobbies
- Webs browsed during work
- Webs browsed during free time
- At what time frame they usually browse and with what purpose?
- Why is it important for you?
- What is the objective of this user in your web?
- What elements does the site have to have to facilitate their journey?
- How will you measure the engagement with the page?

Below there is a persona analysis for the art web esglaiart.es.

Name	Laura Bugo
Job	Teacher
Age	37
Hobbies	Painting
Status	Married, no children
Websites most browsed	artnews.com, techcrunch.com, youtube.com
How they connect	Mobile during the day and tablet by night
What's expected from the web	Shows her art to the world and sell paintings
What should I take into account for her success	Easy to publish paintings since she's very busy. Reminders through email about the page so she can access every now and then
Social media	Facebook and Instagram

Once you know them, it will be easier to design the page, facilitate their way to buy or contact you, and also find automatically the best channels to show them more effective advertising.

COST AND PROFIT PER EVERY CLIENT ACQUISITION

A fundamental part of the online marketing investment will be determined by knowing the return that each invested euro gives back. Therefore, we have to keep in mind from day one how we'll measure success analysing web metrics and what each client is bringing to us, so, investing a large budget in advertising might not be a bad idea as long as it's a positive return.

- What is the average cost for every new user acquired?
- How much on average does the user spend when buying on your website?
- What is the net profit contributed by each new customer?
- Which have been the main sources of traffic and which ones haven't worked?
- How long does the retention of a new customer acquired last?

All answers to the above questions should be known and have positive values in order to have a good business model. And you should even be able to define it through formulas that will help you predict how you'll do in the following months after a defined investment.

Afterwards, you are in a position to decide if you need to change the marketing strategy, the prices or margins of the products or how to retain the clients.

6. HOW CAN A WEBSITE GENERATE INCOME?

For your website being profitable will depend on its reputation, age, number of visits and quality of the content you offer. Be patient with your online income and don't wait for too great results immediately. Your income after 5 years should be much better than the first one. Have a plan and be consistent.

See here some characteristics that impact on the value of your site and its possible online income:

- How established your web is in its industry compared with possible competitors (years that it has been generating traffic, reputation among other bloggers or similar webs that talk about yours and link to it).
- Quality and experience it offers to your users. We are all users, so you already know what you like or don't in a website and what will make you come back to it or look for an alternative. I don't like a web full of ads either.
- The traffic you receive weekly and the followers/fans you have in social media. The higher your traffic and the more followers you have on social media, the more value your page or brand has and it will be considered more 'influential' for people, therefore other brands would pay you to talk about their products.
- And if you have an online store, then your business model will be defined as the rest of the stores: either you sell a lot of volume with little margin, or fewer products but with a high and sufficient margin to compensate you.

MONETIZATION THROUGH CONTENT: FREE AND PAID

Your content should attract visitors, and there's nothing that attracts more visitors than free things, or in other words, there's nothing that causes more rejection than paying for something if they believe they can find it elsewhere for free.

Give away free things, whether information or files, people love it. This will bring more visits to your web and consequently, more brands will be interested in you promoting their products. These can be PDFs of an infographic with a nice design, a PSD (Photoshop file) for those designers or photography lovers, from which they could learn something about how you applied those layers of effects in your photo retouches. Offer free access to a video tutorial that could be part of a course you offer as a consultant in your specialty.

The part where they pay for the content can come later. They have to want to continue with this course they already tried for free and are willing to pay to download the following PDFs, access to the videos or simply hire you. Many income streams can come after you've given things away.

I remember all those applications I downloaded for free but ended up paying for their *pro* version to have all those extended capabilities that the free one didn't have. And the good thing was that I already knew what I was paying for: the app that I liked using, plus what limited me.

Perhaps, I could've found another free app offering the same thing, but I'm used to this one, and why? because I tried it for free! So you see why giving out things for free works like magic?

ADVERTISING ON YOUR WEB PAGES: DISPLAY AND GOOGLE ADSENSE

One of the most typical ways of monetizing a web page is placing ads through your contents. However, you'll have to get a lot of traffic so you can really get income through advertising.

The challenge will be to find the right balance between the number of ads shown in your page in very big and top placements for advertisers to wish to show their ads on your web and not to put too many as it becomes less attractive and the ads wouldn't stand out that much anymore between too much noise.

And on the flip side, you'll be getting worse the experience that the visitors will have in your web since you'll be adding difficulties and distractions for them in finding their way through the information and conversion. And lastly, if they click on the ads and it opens that link in the same window tab, it means that your users will be leaving your website.

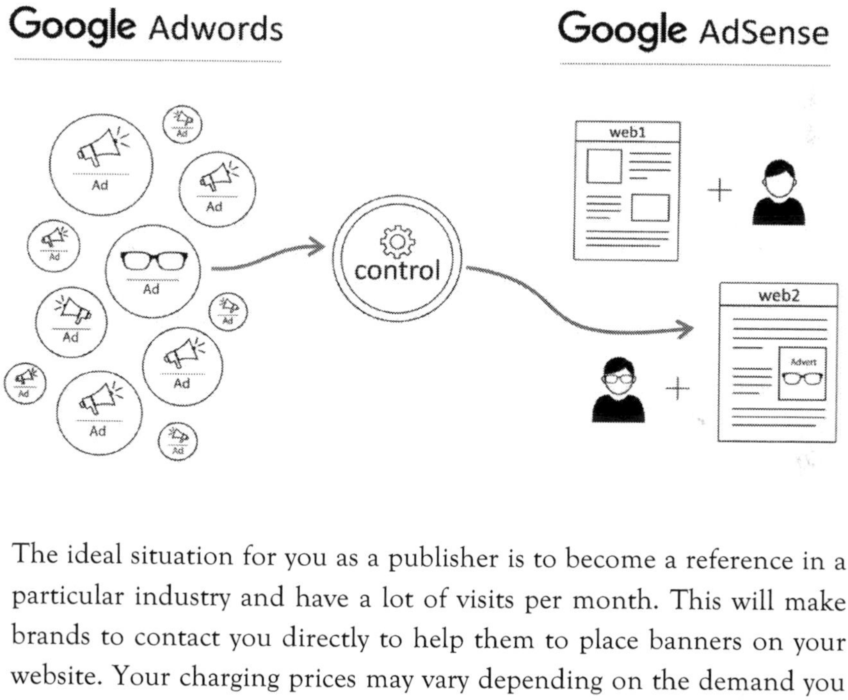

The ideal situation for you as a publisher is to become a reference in a particular industry and have a lot of visits per month. This will make brands to contact you directly to help them to place banners on your website. Your charging prices may vary depending on the demand you have.

Perhaps, advertisers knocking on our door isn't always the case for most of us and even more when we're starting with our first websites. However, we could always use the ad server form Google: AdSense.

Google AdSense provides you with some small 'frames' or 'windows' of different sizes which you can choose from and place them throughout your web without knowing with certainty what they'll show at a specific time or to one of your customers.

Google will be responsible for choosing from their advertising program Google AdWords, whose ad, from among all their advertisers, is the best to be shown on your website to one of your particular visitors at a particular moment. The ad is related to your content, and interestingly also works with their cookies (which determines users' interests, search history, etc.).

As you can see on the previous example, the user who has been researching glasses and Google knows this information because of user's Google Chrome browser so an advertisement for opticians is chosen to display an ad for glasses, as it may be very relevant for that user.

The first thing you have to do in Google AdSense is to register or sign in with the Gmail account that you use for any other Google service clicking to: https://www.google.es/adsense/start/

And in two simple steps, by providing information about your page and its content, you'll be ready to start.

To get started, you will have to create a new 'Ad Unit' clicking on 'My ads', and 3 different type of ads will be presented. The easiest for you to get ads on your site right away will be the first, 'Text & Display ads' but it's worth exploring the others later on.

When creating an ad unit (that window you'll place in your web to show ads), you'll be able to choose different configuration parameters.

They are:

- Size: first you'll have to decide where it will go in your web, but for example, if you're thinking about a large horizontal one on the header or even close to your logo and main menu, then you can choose the 790x90px. A good move is to choose the 'Responsive' one, so Google will show whichever ad fits that space.
- Ad type: Image, rich media or text. Here you'll be indicating to Google if you allow to show any ad format on your placements or you'd rather exclude rich media, since you wouldn't want animations on your home page if the brand tries to show serious content. Remember that you can't control everything that will be displayed and you just rely on Google and its quality to filter bad ads.
- Text ads format: Those ad spaces may not only show banners, but also text ads that come from AdWords, and through this option you can choose how you want them to look embedded in your web, choosing the colour of the text title, description, button and link. In this way, you'll be able to show those ads with a more integrated look and they'll seem to be part of your own content, therefore a lot of users will click more; or they can look totally contrasted from the harmony of the web, trying to attract attention and get more clicks in that way. Remember, be honest with your visitors by showing them what's an ad and what's not. There's no formula to know what works best for your site, so you just have to test.

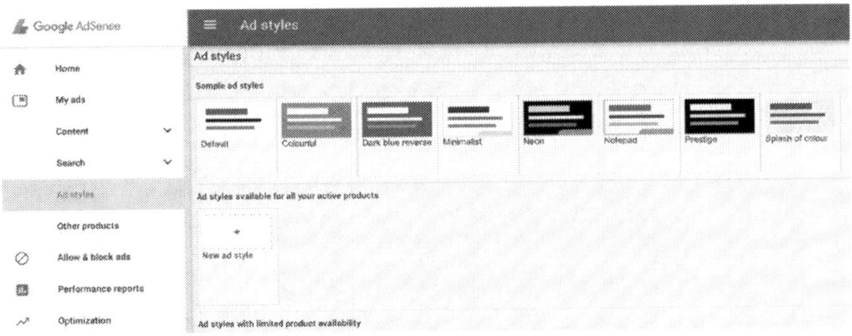

Once you have it all set up, a code will be generated and you need to place it wherever you want it to appear on your website and how you want it to be shown.

If your website is on WordPress (and I'll show you how to do it in the next section), you'll only have to go to the page where you want to show the ads, and in the text editor select the 'html' tab and paste the code there.

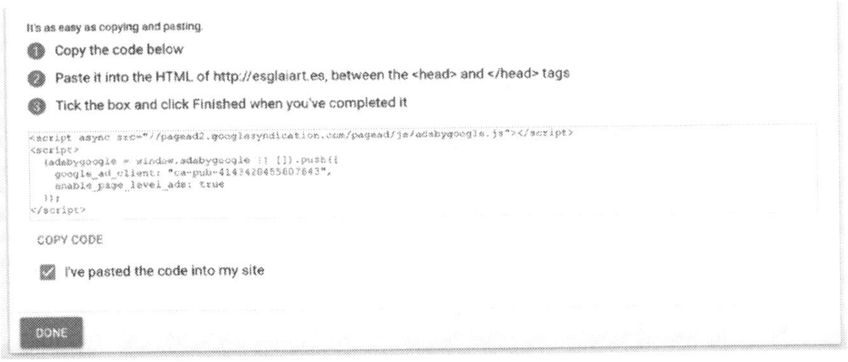

In the image below, you can see an example in one of the art sites I like to visit, and the ad displayed there is about suits rather than art.

I'm seeing this ad because I was buying shirts online from another brand, and Google knowing this decided to target me with these ads, so they are relevant to me, even though it has nothing to do with art or the website itself. This is great because imagine if this website was yours, you wouldn't like to show ads from competitors but rather adverts that are likely to get clicks and make you some dollars

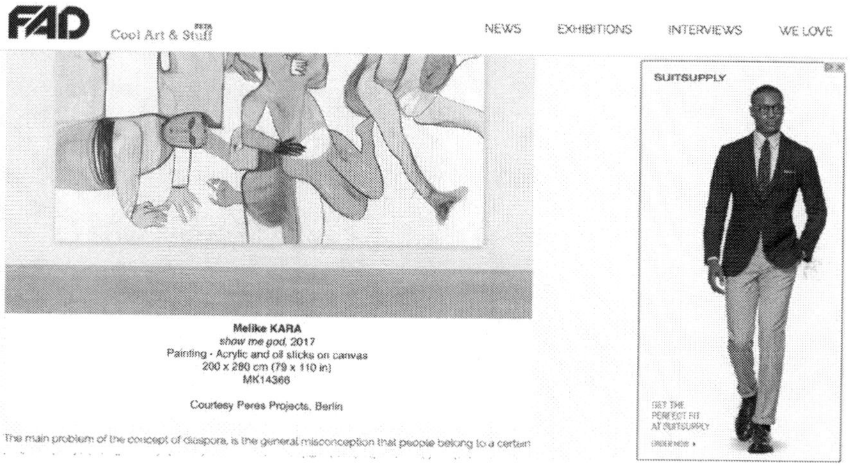

7. CREATING A SUCCESSFUL ONLINE STORE

91% of the purchases are still made offline, but the annual increase in online purchases by every European country is very significant: 9% in Spain and 11% as the European average. And more than half of the people that finished their purchase in a physical store, visited the ecommerce or interacted with the seller's website in the first place.

If you have a product inventory to sell, whether you have a physical store or not, your online presence is mandatory since the number of customers that can visit you in your city' address is much smaller compared to the number of visitors you can have on your website from all over the country, and even beyond.

This section covers how to successfully operate the mechanism of an online store with products that can be bought directly. Since you now know how you can generate money online, now we only have to get ourselves ready to do it in the best way.

KNOW YOUR PRODUCT PROFIBILITY IN DETAIL

It's important that you know the products you want to sell and the challenges they have, so in case that you're still thinking about it, take into account these points which may be key to make your logistics or make your maintenance more expensive.

Profit margins for each product

Your online store or ecommerce will be mainly based on products that fit in one of these two income streams:

- You can sell a high volume of products and the margins are small per unit.
- You can sell fewer products but your profit for each one will be much higher.

You must know how much profit every unit generates: both the gross profit (your selling price minus its raw cost for you) as well as the net profit (subtracting also the proportional cost of your warehouse rental, your employees, electricity, etc.).

Can they be sent through the post easily?

Your level of sales and costs will be determined by the volume, weight and packaging of your products, as well as the maximum distance where they can be distributed to.

It's not the same if you want to sell leather wallets to all of the UK, which you can pack and send in a very attractive envelope, versus selling furniture online, like beds or mattresses which volume and weight could be quite a challenge to store and also to deliver.

Will you allow returns and refunds?

When selling online, you have to reduce any possible headache or mistrust from the buyer, therefore I recommend you consider that the buyer will have the possibility to return and get refunded for your products if they're not satisfied, and that will be a risk (and potential cost) you have to take into account; as well as – some products – should offer a guarantee for some years.

This also means that if you think your products can't be returned once they've been delivered for any reason (hygiene, quality, etc.), then you could have more difficulties selling them online.

How much will every user spend with you?

Think about whether your clients tend to buy more than one item when they visit your online store or if the purchases tend to be more individual.

Additionally, will they buy more from you after some time? If you sell a bed, the client will probably make an order for one single item once. But if you're a supermarket, they will buy several products and when they use them, they could come back for more, therefore their loyalty is very important.

What is your unique value proposition (UVP) or unique selling point (USP)?

Your item has to be distinguished and beat your competition. If it's a homemade product, it won't be hard to achieve uniqueness and you'll have your own brand; but if you sell products manufactured by others, then you have to differentiate by offering a unique experience to your customers using your website and with your delivery, their refunds, your customer service, gifts or discounts among others.

This is even more important if those products are sold in bigger online marketplaces like Amazon, Etsy or eBay. Although those are websites where you could also sell, you'll have to compete aggressively with price; but if you do sell through them, encourage your customers to buy directly from you next time.

8. SELL YOUR PRODUCTS ON AMAZON

HOW AMAZON WORKS

Amazon is the king of ecommerce, both here as well as in America. You only need to see their constant lines of innovation to know that they won't stop growing. Amazon knows that local proximity is no longer a decisive factor for users to buy and the online platforms are rapidly ending with many physical stores that keep storing stock.

I see Amazon as something additional to our physical and to our online store. It's simply somewhere we also need to be, since many of our users will look there in the first place. They will evaluate and compare your product. They know most of the product reviews are found there, therefore having presence in Amazon and taking care of the reviews will be very important for your success.

Amazon has a different business model than most; it doesn't make money for the sale of products (besides most aren't their products nor are distributed by them). Their business model is in the paid subscriptions of the users that want faster deliveries or more content like books or show TVs. As they say, people use a website for two reasons: either to save money or time. The users already know that in Amazon they'll always find the most competitive prices in the market, so they only make the effort to save some time.

Or in case of the sellers, Amazon don't add a commission for the sale of products from other stores or users, but using their logistics and warehouses to storage products. Their main objective is to have the highest possible volume of traffic on their site, get the largest number of members and build a giant database to be able to use it in their new products, similar to Google or Facebook.

SELLING ON AMAZON

If you want to sell on Amazon, you'll have to access to sellercentral.amazon.com and subscribe through a small payment of £0,75/month to sell less than 40 products a month or £25/month if you intend to sell more than that with additional advantages like being able to create new listings in the Amazon categories, so if your products are inventions not yet catalogued, this option would be good for you.

If the product already exists in their catalogue, you don't have to do anything more than select it and compete with the minimum offer to increase your sales options.

Once your account has been created, you'll be able to gain access to the Amazon seller interface and put your products on sale manually, being in charge of uploading all the information, optimizing the text so it can be found easier during a search, and the most important part, the distribution of the product when it's sold.

Delivery of products

There are two possibilities for you when it comes to logistic and distribution of your products. You can be in charge of packaging your product either at home or your store and sending it to the address provided, which can be a good option if you also have a physical store and wants to encourage your customers to buy from you directly and if the estimated sales volume per month is small and you want to save some money from Amazon on their commission dispatching and storing the products.

The other option would be using Amazon's logistics and all their storage and distribution channels (FBA - Fulfilment by Amazon), which is a system more appropriate for sellers with larger volumes and in a short amount of time. Once you've created your products in the same interface, you have to send the inventory to the address given by Amazon so they can store and deliver them according to the demand.

This system is highly recommended for items that will be sold in large volumes like books, so you would prefer to send a large package to the Amazon warehouses than individual packages to the buyers even though you lose a little of that personal touch you could add in each delivered package.

OPTIMIZE YOUR PRODUCT LISTINGS TO GET MORE VIEWS

Amazon is one of the most used search engines in the world, behind Google or YouTube, and it's n°1 for product searches.

The traffic in Amazon is so large because of a lot of people start their search directly in Amazon and their product range and categories keep expanding and attracting new customers.

As a good search engine, it also uses algorithms to sort their results when a user makes a search, and it's important to know the most relevant points for optimization and organic positioning in Amazon (aka SEO in Amazon):

1. **Title**: the title in Amazon has to describe the product in 100 characters, highlighting the most important aspects of the product, like the brand, model or something that differentiates it from the other results, since it will be the key to getting a click but don't forget to add the search terms that users will insert in

the search bar. 100 characters' title is a long title, so make the most of it.

2. **Traffic:** the more visits your product has, the more it will be taken into account for the following visualization in another search.
3. **Description:** Amazon has different lines to describe the product. The optimal practice is to add between 3 and 5 short, concise and detailed descriptions, again using relevant keywords.
4. **Reviews:** It's been studied and proved that having reviews in Amazon is a clear differentiating feature between products when it comes to getting the click. Note that I said 'having reviews', without specifying if they're positive or negative, since it's better to have negative ones than not have at all (which can indicate that no one has bought it). Obviously, the more reviews you have and more positive these are, your sale options will increase exponentially as well as the opportunity to appear in the first results. If you launch a new product and want to incentivise the users to write the first reviews, which are the ones that count the most, you can join their program 'Vine Reviews', where you give away free products to those users chosen by Amazon as the ones that evaluate more products, and they will write a review, but be careful, because no one guarantees it will be a good one.

STEP 2

WEB DEVELOPMENT AND ECOMMERCE

9. BUYING YOUR HOSTING AND DOMAIN

This is where the knowledge of a webmaster is relevant. When you pay someone to develop your website, it's because of your fear or inability to purchase, install, and configure hosting and a domain.

You know how you want the final result to be, but taking the first step to get there seems really complex. Don't worry, I will show you how to do it step by step, and once you overcome this stage, creating websites for your businesses or clients will be simple and easy.

WHAT IS A HOSTING AND WHAT IS ITS RELATIONSHIP WITH THE DOMAIN?

When we talk about a web page, we tend to think that we are talking about something that starts with http://www.nameweb.es, however, it is just a domain (a direction that points us to a place where the files and data of that web is hosted and will be visualised in your screen). These files are stored in a hosting provider, also known as server.

The hosting that you will buy is like a house big enough, not only to have the files of one website, but for several. Just imagine that every website is hosted in each room.

Also, imagine that these rooms have separate doors to access them directly from the outside. These gateways are the domains and is how our users visit our site.

The following image shows a possible hosting you buy from a provider like 1and1, and as an example, imagine that you have 3 of your webs in them, all completely different among each other and you still have some free space in case you have another online idea.

As you can see, when people enter through the domain1 (freshfoodcali.com) in their browser, they are sent to where the website1 files are located (the files of freshfoodcali.com). So basically, the two things you need to buy to have a web are these: a domain and a hosting.

The cost of the hosting you buy depends on the visits to your website. If you want to launch a new idea or product and you are not sure how the market will react, or if you are a local business that simply needs to have a good online presence to compete in Google with other companies, then you don't need to make a very strong initial investment with the server, since you can always increase it afterwards when necessary.

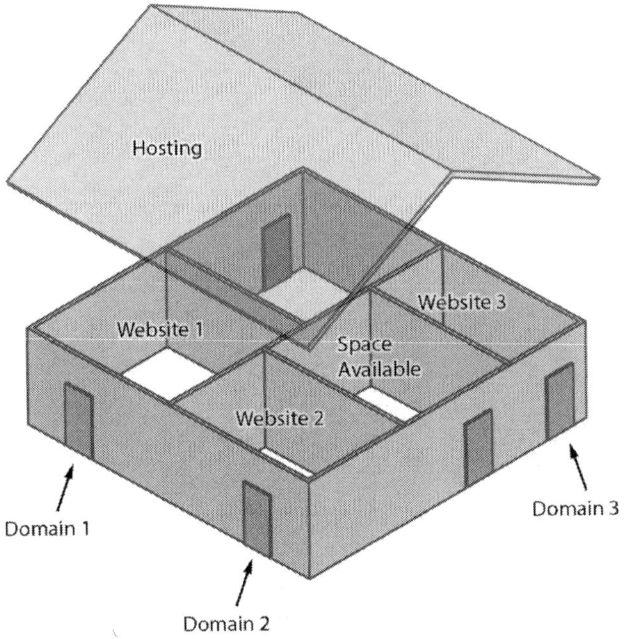

However, if you are a big brand, you will need a more expensive and more specialised hosting product. In fact, if you own a big company, you would need a team of specialists for each of the sections of this book.

Dedicated vs. Shared Hosting

When you buy a cheaper hosting (they are the 'shared' ones), your house (or your hosting) is located within a larger community in which certain resources are distributed among all the 'houses'.

All visitors want to go to different rooms or webs, but they will have to go in through a common main door, and the width of that door is limited (also known as the hosting bandwidth).

When you are deciding which hosting to buy, you will see that buying a dedicated hosting is more expensive, although much faster and more efficient. And to keep the comparison, it is as if you had a house of your own and all the traffic that arrives, access your website without problems, quickly and without limit of visits.

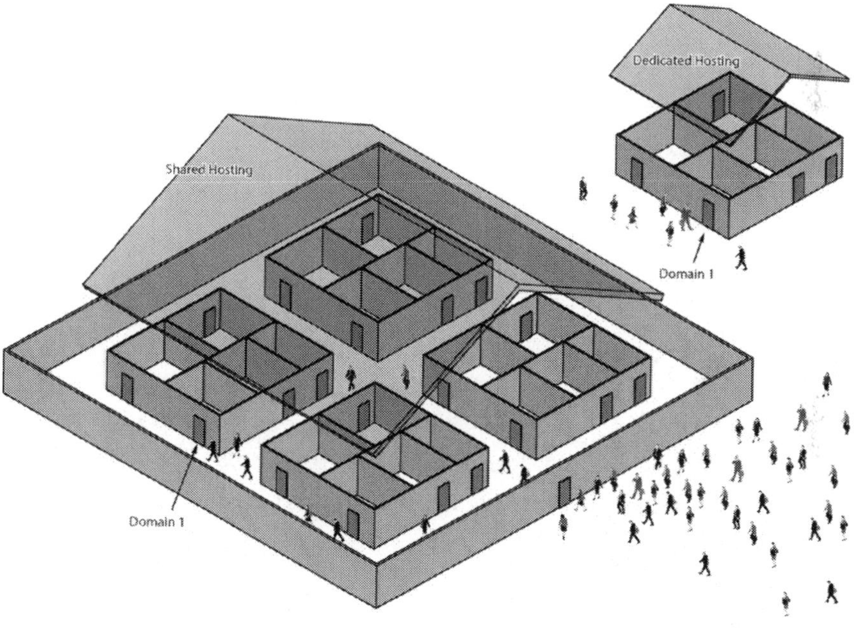

CHOOSING AND BUYING A HOSTING

If you want, you can stop here and digest what I just explained. The best way is to start your research as if you were going to buy one. Check out some of these hosting providers and their offerings:

- 1and1.com
- godaddy.com
- BlueHost.com
- Hostgator.com

There are many hosting providers and I'm not interested to advertise any in particular, since I have not worked with all of them, so I wouldn't be fair, but with a couple of minutes spent in Google researching, you'll get a good idea which of them suits you best.

With those I worked with and being in a position to advise you on, one that is easy and intuitive, with good customer service, and easy administrator dashboard in several languages is 1and1. The control panel shown in the following image is for you to get an idea how it looks.

Also, bear in mind that it is a provider chosen by many people, so if you choose the cheapest version of hosting, you may not have the best experience or web speed.

Some tips for choosing your provider:

- Domains included: Although they can be bought separately and with different providers, I would suggest buying the domain at the same time that you buy the hosting since they will offer you deals to encourage you to buy both and I also think that it is an advantage at the time of setting it all up. Therefore, don't rush to choose the hosting until you have decided the name of your domain and take advantage of the purchase.
- Nº of databases: Whichever you choose, it will come with at least one, but it is important to choose a hosting with more databases as perhaps in the future you will want to create new webs or applications and you need a new database for every one. *Think: one database per room.*
- Web space: Defined in Gigabytes (GB), it will be the capacity of your web space, or as I compared before, how big the house where

you store your webs would be. The more space you have, the more webs you can store in it.

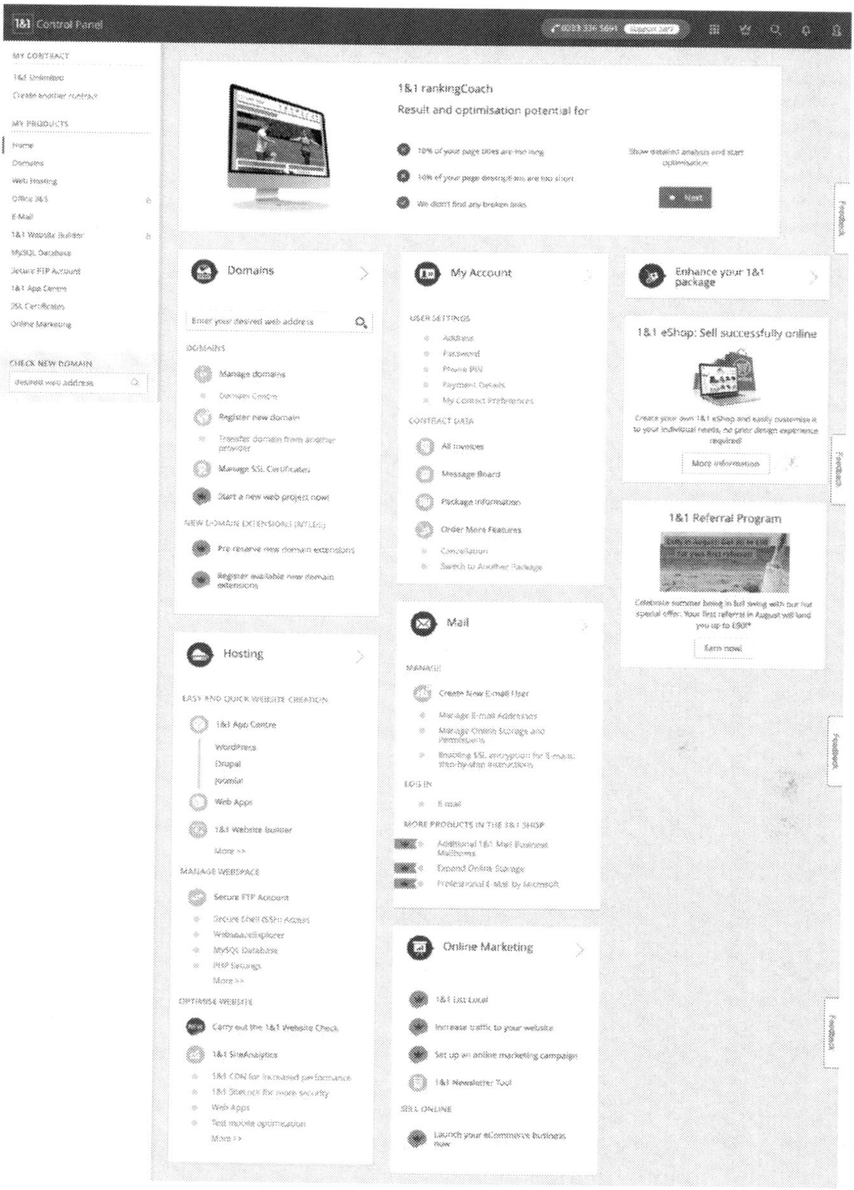

- RAM Memory: This is the memory dedicated for all visitors and your hosting and where the most repeated code instructions and most commonly downloaded files will be stored, so that access to your web is faster for the majority of your new visitors. The greater the memory, the better.
- Linux or Windows: you will see that all providers offer you these two options and Linux is the option that you have to choose as operating system of your web since it is the most recognised by web servers. Those who choose Windows are those who don't understand and think it has to do with the Windows they have on their computer, or on the flip side, professionals who know that there are specific characteristics of your website and code that must be executed by the Windows server.

CHOOSING AND BUYING A DOMAIN

The domain chosen will also be a fundamental part of your online strategy and it is a very cheap one.

It is recommended that you buy it from the same hosting provider, since it will be easier for you to set it up, although this may not offer the extension of the domain you want and thus you may prefer to buy it elsewhere. This is not a problem.

The most common domain providers are:

- 1and1.es
- godaddy.com
- name.com

The best considerations for choosing your domain:

- It has to be easy for users to remember it: The shorter and easier to remember, the better. People need to be able to remember the name of your website in a conversation and invite others to visit your page, without having to find your business card or email. A good example for an online marketing consultancy could be consulting.digital or a short name for an app like Uber.

- You have to have, if not all, some keywords to help with search engine ranking: as in the example of boatstoragemallorca.com, the goal when choosing this domain is to match some of the most searched words in Google with your business offering, in this case, to storage your boat during winter.
- If your business is also physical and you want to keep your brand, then your domain should respect that.
- If your web is going to have content in different languages, it is best to get a domain that does not contain keywords in only one of the language, but instead is aligned with a brand name, such as Lynda.com.

Choosing the extension of your domain: .com, .uk or others.

This will depend on your activity and where your audience is. If it is a web in several languages, with an audience from all over the world, a .com extension would be the most appropriate.

But if your activity is very specific and there is an extension related to it, you could use it for your users to associate it very quickly, for example, Cristams.hotel, tells you it is either a hotel or a hotel chain.

Acquiring domains is cheap and I think for the security reasons, it is convenient to buy different options of it, so that competitors don't take advantage of your potential traffic.

But don't get obsessed buying .com, .co.uk, .de, .hotel, .org, .me and .info as it will not be necessary and what it's important is to focus on one and that one becomes recognised as your brand. If you plan for your page to compete very strongly in a single market, you should definitely use the extension of that country, such as .es for Spain or .de for Germany.

You can find a complete list of domain extensions at this link: http://www.iana.org/domains/root/db

Check the availability of your domain

When you have in mind some possibilities, I recommend that you go to the internet to check if they already exist, which will help you to discard or maybe to choose another final extension for it that you didn't consider as your first option.

To check if it is available, you just have to go to any provider of domains listed above and enter it in their search bar. They will ask you which domain you want, to see if it is available and you can buy it with them if it is.

I prefer to use a little more generic or global website to search for availability of my domain because sometimes when you go to a provider, it only shows you if it is available with them. For example, on 1and1.es, you will not be able to see or buy German domains.

A good way to start your research is in www.name.com/domain/search/and enter the domain you would like, displaying a list about its availability, but not only the one you want, but also different variations of extension so you may find out one that works even better or choose an alternative one in case yours is not available.

Instructions to link your domain with your hosting being both from different suppliers

You could find yourself in this situation for several reasons: You have bought a hosting, but you did not find the domain in the same provider with the extension that you were looking for, or maybe you have bought the website and its domain to another company or webmaster. I cannot give you much details on the step-by-step process and show you screenshots for all possible combinations and providers, but I will put you on the right path on the actions you must take:

1. Go to the domain provider and find the DNS configuration, where you will find a CNAME, MX, DNS1, DNS2 labels.
2. Access the control panel of your hosting, where you will have the web hosted and in your domains section, click add a new one. You will have several options, but you must select the one to link an external domain.
3. Configure it manually and enter the information that you found in point 1.
4. Wait a couple of minutes and the domain should point to your new hosting address. You may be required to utilise a code as a verification measure.

The CNAME is the version of your domain with the subdomain www. MX records are configurations for your email to work with the external domain, but only when using the email service from your hosting provider, which is where you have memory to store your emails. The domain alone is nothing else than a name.

10. WEB DEVELOPMENT WITH WORDPRESS

DOWNLOAD AND INSTALLATION

At this point, you should have a better idea about who your audience is, what you want to achieve, domain chosen and a hosting bought. Great progress! Let's develop the website now!

WordPress is the CMS (content management system) solution that has given me the best results in web development and for online businesses. Its advantages are:

- It's free.
- You increase its potential with plugins (or software extensions), most of them also for free and 1-click install, which would be like the apps on your mobile that add different functionalities to it.
- Change designs with different templates with a very low budget and a perfectly professional and optimised result.
- Offers solutions for any type of web page, such as business services, ecommerce, social networks, product downloads, directory, booking system, etc.
- You can have your web in several languages easily.
- You can automatically optimise many factors that affect the Google rankings without additional cost.

FULL PROCESS TO DEVELOP YOUR WEB

Don't confuse WordPress to create webs (CMS) with the blog system of WordPress.com. We will focus on the former, which is found and downloaded in the following URL: WordPress.org.

For the installation of the web, it will be necessary that you have already purchased a web hosting and preferably also the domain, although if you don't have it, you can always use the *system domain* offered by the hosting provider.

The next image will be helpful for you to visualise the whole process, since you can do several things in parallel, which I'll be explaining one by one along the chapter.

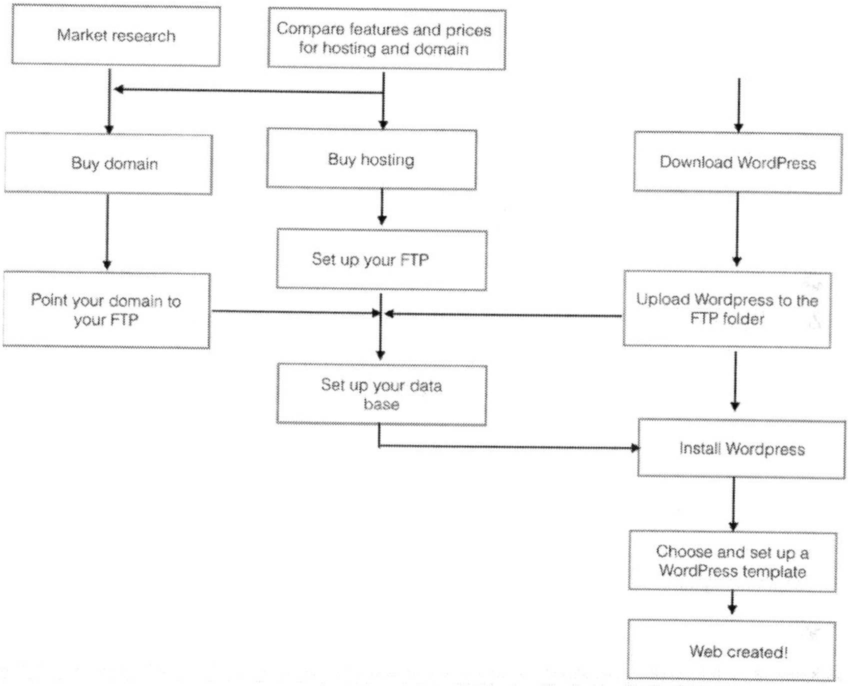

FTP SET UP TO ACCESS TO YOUR BACK-END

What is an FTP and what do I need it for?

Once you have the hosting purchased (your hosting or house explained above), you will have to know how to access the backend, where you will store and modify the files of your web constantly. However, you have to learn a way to not enter through the main door (the domain) since when the web is active that door is the entrance for your visitors to your beautiful store or web, so we are going to build a 'back door' where you have the files and documents stored. This access is done via FTP (Files Transfer Protocol). The web or final visible product by the users through your domain is called front-end and when you work and manage web files or edit the content, we will be referring to the back-end.

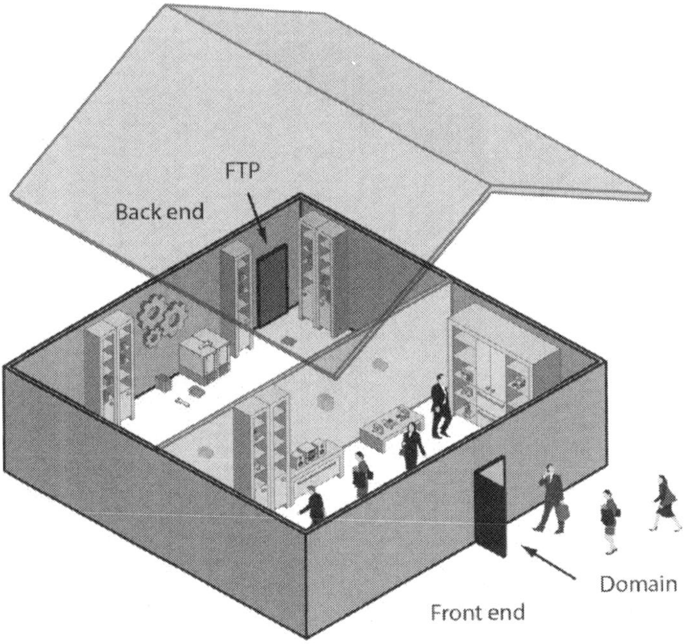

Access to your FTP to view your web files

Step 1

Access the control panel of your provider, either 1and1, Bluehost, or any other and locate the FTPs section. You can find it by searching for FTP Access or File Management.

Step 2

Create a new FTP connection and it will provide you the following information. Don't leave without it:

Server: Many times, it is simply your domain (in the case of 1and1), although there are many others in which an ftp. or ftp@ is added in front of it.

User: It will be an alphanumeric combination.

Password: The one you have chosen when creating the new FTP connection.

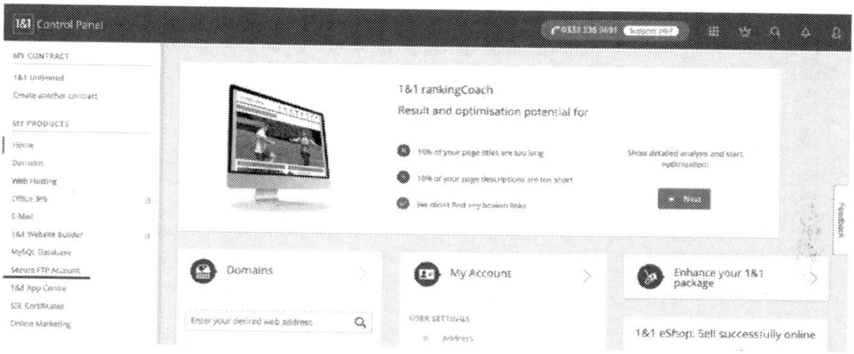

Step 3

Now you have to download a program that allows you to access that backend via FTP and view your web as a system of folders and files like your computer.

This software is free and there are several options, but I recommend FileZilla (for any system) or Yummy FTP (for Mac only).

Once installed, open the program and enter the 3 values you obtained in the previous step (server, username and password) in their respective boxes, followed by a click on 'Quick Connect'.

You will see the main screen with different divisions where normally on the left you have the files from your computer and on the right the online web files where you have just accessed.

You can easily drag files from one place to another, uploading or downloading files between your computer and the web server.

This is how we will upload the WordPress folders to our FTP root directory.

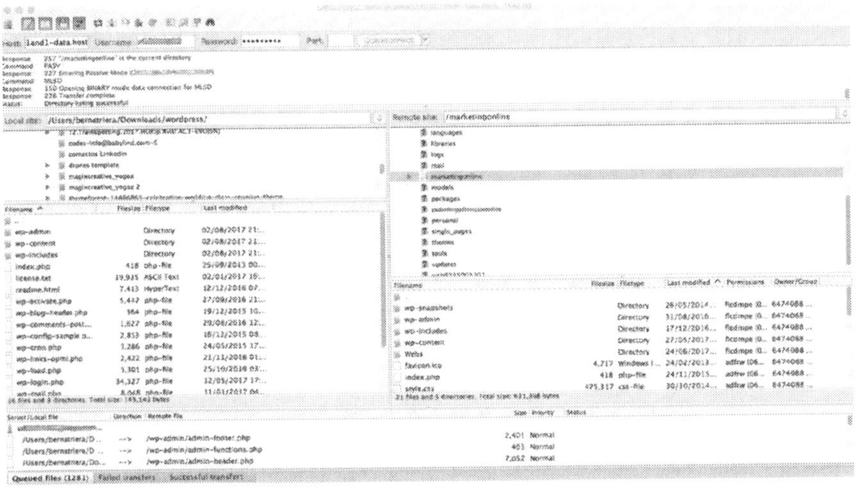

CREATE A DATABASE FOR YOUR WEB

The database of a web will be very important to enable you to create content and data flow between the web and the users. The database would be like the shelves of that backroom where we will place the folders and documents, so that they are easily found whenever needed.

You only need one database per website and as we did for the FTP, we will create a new database from the control panel of your hosting provider. On this occasion, you should find a section of database or MySQL. In the previous screenshot from 1and1, you will find it just above the FTP access, called MySQL Database.

Clicking on this option will show you the ones you have available and the option to create new ones. Create a new one and be sure to put a complicated password that you will only need once when installing

WordPress.

Once it's created and after a few minutes after its configuration, you will get the following information. Copy it somewhere, since you will have to use it during the installation. These parameters are:

- Name of the database
- User of the database
- Server of the database
- Password

UPLOADING AND SETTING UP WORDPRESS IN YOUR WEB

Great, now we have access to the backend (FTP) and we have placed the shelves (Database). Now, we only need to start uploading the WordPress content to be closer to have a functional website.

To download and upload WordPress folders to your web space, follow these simple steps:

1. Download the latest version of the WordPress files which you will find at www.wordpress.org.

   In a couple of minutes, you will have downloaded a file that when unzipped will have a folder called WordPress, which will be full of other subfolders and files, which will be basically your initial website structure and once online, almost functional.
2. Upload all these files and subfolders to your web online through the FTP program you have downloaded (FileZilla for example) and connect the session with your hosting, clicking to a 'QuickConnect'.
3. Once connected, locate on the left hand side (your computer), where you have the WordPress files and subfolders (from the folder 'WordPress') and to the right, you can see that there is a folder or a file, you can ignore that and create a new folder that

you will name as you want related to your site, i.e. 'webrestaurant'.

4. Drag all the content from inside your WordPress folder from the left (all subfolders and files) into the 'webrestaurant' folder on the right and wait for the uploading process to be completed.
5. Once your web is ready inside your online folder 'webrestaurant' is the moment that we open the main entrance door through the domain using any of our web browsers, like Google Chrome, but just before this, we must ensure from the control panel of our hosting that our domain points to that new folder we just created.

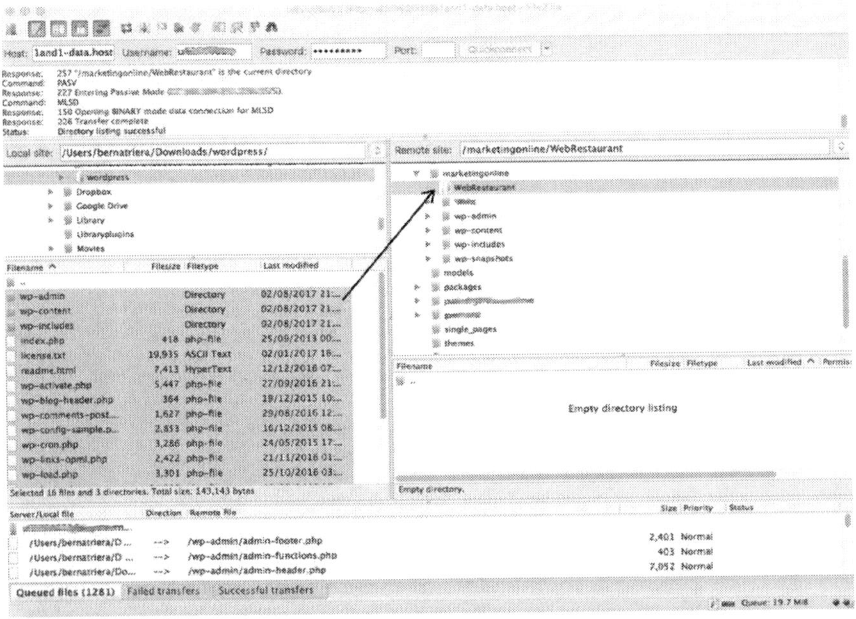

6. Go to the domains section and edit the destination of the domain which will point to the root online folder by default. Select the folder online we created /webrestaurant/. It may take a few minutes for the change to take effect.

7. The process will be completed when you enter the URL in the browser (myrestaurant.co.uk) and the following window of installation of WordPress opens, where you select the language and set up the database with the 4 information points that you have obtained previously (Name of the database, user, server and password). You will also be asked for a table prefix that is wp_ by default, although I usually change it to two more relevant letters to my web, for example in this case, mr_.

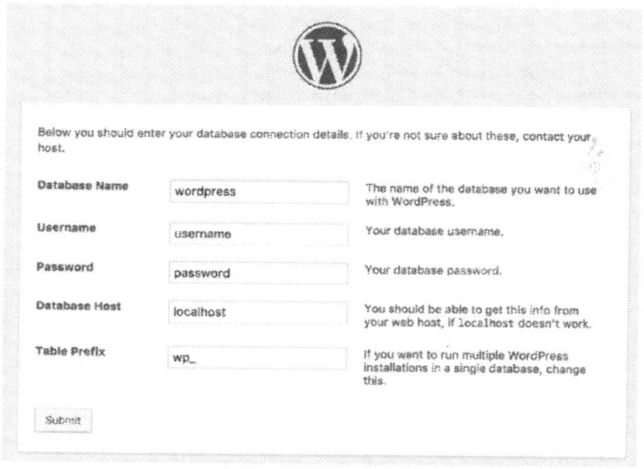

8. When you continue, WordPress will confirm that everything is properly configured and you will only have to enter what your new access to the web will be. Choose a username and password that is complex, but that you can easily remember as it will be the most used one moving forward.

9. All should be ready and introducing myrestaurant.co.uk in the browser will open the default WordPress website.
10. If you want to access the backend of your website, you can do it through myrestaurant.co.uk/wp-admin/.

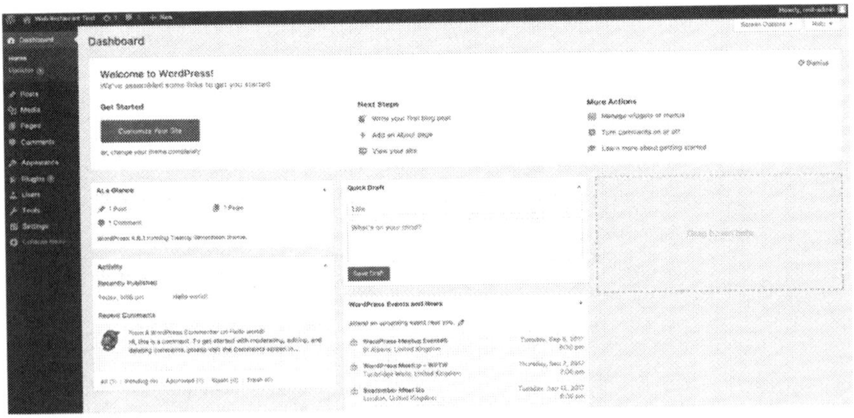

11. WEB DESIGN THROUGH TEMPLATES AND PLUGINS

When I started to develop webs, I understood that in the online world, it is very important to be fast, versatile and give the best impression. It would have taken me ages to learn how to develop a website in HTML5, CSS, and JavaScript's and everything that builds them to create a professional web that I can acquire for $40 in seconds in a WordPress templates store.

Think about what your time is worth and how you want to spend it. For me, the important thing is to focus on the online businesses, its strategy with SEO ranking and advertising to get an economic return, so paying for work that others know how to do much better than I do, it's a smart decision.

The WordPress you just installed is the body (skeleton and skin) of your website. Templates, also known as themes, are its appearance, dress, style, functionality and user experience in it.

The most popular source to buy great templates is themeforest.com and in the menu, you will find a specific section for WordPress templates.

Here, you will have to filter a lot. Try it and research a little before you buy, although I will guide you a little on how to simplify your search.

CHOOSING THE BEST TEMPLATE FOR YOU BUSINESS

Here, I present my tricks on choosing a winning template:

Use filters, but not by category since a good web for your company could be in different ones, like creative, buddypress, etc, but by year created. Choose recent ones if you want some not owned by many people and look modern. Or older ones, so that they are probably more robust and already improved over time. Check their reviews, number of times downloaded and their prices, among others.

Once you have the first list of templates that you want to evaluate, click on one to open its full detailed page with features, comments, and a link to the 'live demo' where you can see it in action. And it's at this stage that I look at a few things to make my decision:

Version number: My recommendation is to analyse how many versions of the template have already been released by its developers from the time they launched and when it was last updated. You can find this out by scrolling down until you find the update log.

If the template has been for sale for many years and it didn't get an update for a while, that indicates that this template is no longer one of the priorities of the developer, so if something is wrong with the code, they may not correct it quickly.

Reviews: See how many downloads this template has had and its total rating. Remember, it is more reliable 4 stars of 12,000 people who have bought it than 5 stars of 20 people.

Comments: I am very interested in looking at the comments tab for two reasons: 1) How many comments it has, to know that maybe it is difficult to change parts of it or it is not very intuitive so people need help. 2) How quickly the developer answers the problems and with which tone or detail. It does not matter if it is complex while you have a good technical support that answers in less than a day.

Features: This will depend on what your page needs and what plugins it should be compatible with. For example, make sure that if you want a social community on your page, your template has the 'buddy press' plugin or similar built-in. In the same way, if you want an online store, the template should incorporate 'WooCommerce'. If you want a page with different languages, the template will have to be prepared to install a language plugin named 'WPML'.

Price: I don’t think it's the most relevant factor, they're all between $35-

$55, so focus more on what you really need and gives you the least amount of work.

Live Demo: You go to the demo and navigate through the page as if you were a user, a client of yours, not you as a developer. Check out the following:

- Navigation menu: Do you like its position, how does it display drop menus, etc.?
- Home page: Do you like its structure, functionality, images, slider?
- They usually offer different versions of the home page from which you can choose the design you like most with a simple click.
- Individual pages: See the structure of the content, images, font used, colours and sizes, although you will be able to change all these later on.
- Online store: if you want an online store, display how the product list is shown, and click on a specific product, how much information does it show? How many pictures? Reviews, comments, buttons to buy, compare, add to cart or to the wish list?.
- Blog: How it shows the latest posts, ease to filter them, etc.
- Team: If you need to show the members of your team, make sure that the template has a section for the team, with images, descriptions and individual contact details.
- Portfolio: If you are interested in showing your customers your latest services or jobs, this section must be on your template before you buy it.
- Contact: Is it how you would like your users to see your contact information? The form fields can be changed, but in general, do you like how the map and information are being displayed?

With WordPress, we put to our web the body, going from nothing to a functional web. The template was the dress, giving it its image and main look. The plugins that you are going to see below would represent the complements like the watch, shoes, glasses, ... to add additional functionalities. Plugins will give a whole variety of skills and added value to your web for free.

Over time, you will see that most of the things you would like your website to do, other developers have already thought and created it for free for you.

Plugins must first be installed and subsequently activated. You can have them installed without having them active, which will be very useful if you have a problem one day and you want to check if something that you have recently activated is incompatible with your template or another plugin.

How to add a plugin?

To add a plugin, you have two options:

Easy and free: Go to the 'plugins' section of the admin menu from the left hand side of your WordPress (access via myweb.co.uk/wp-admin) and select 'add new'.

Browse the suggested ones or search in your search bar with keywords like ‘social’ and once you explore the different options offered, click on install. Once installed, you should activate it to make it to work and configure it.

Paid: There are plugins that you have to pay and you will not find them in the catalogue of WordPress, but you can Google them to find the right solution.

Once you find it, pay and download the zip file to your computer and then from WordPress, in the same 'add new' section, select this time

'Upload file' and select the zip file.

Plugins are just subfolders inside the online root folder of your website i.e. webrestaurant/wp-content/plugins/ and there you can upload or delete them via FTP. It's very useful if one day a plugin blocks the web completely and you cannot even gain access to the backend to uninstall it.

10 Plugins You Must Know

1) W3 Total Cache

It is one of the best plugin to handle the cache of your web page. Cache is a memory that helps to load web pages faster.

When you visit a web page, it installs certain elements in your computer's cache which will make the next time you access the same site faster, since those items will be pre-downloaded.

The problem for developers is that when we make changes to our pages, visitors could continue to see old content, but this plugin will help us to empty the stored cache and ask the computers to reload all the files of our website.

It also has additional functions such as GZIP compression, which allows you to transfer and load pages faster between servers and browsers through a compression protocol and decompression between terminals, all done automatically, so don't worry.

To quickly empty the cache after making several changes, simply click on 'Performance' / 'Purge all Caches' from the new tab called 'Performance' in the upper horizontal bar of your WordPress administration panel.

2) All in one SEO or Yoast SEO

This is the second plugin I install to all my web pages in WordPress. There are many developers who prefer Yoast SEO, although I have become accustomed to 'All in one SEO' and as long as it is compatible with templates and plugins, I use that.

The two do their job, which is to allow you to personalise with a title, description and other SEO ranking features of all your content, like all pages, products or blog posts.

In the general options, you can configure to generate titles and automatic descriptions from the name of the blog or web, author, date, category or description, although the best use for a good positioning is to write each title and description individually, that is, just leave in the title %page_title% and in the description %description% which means that you will take into account the title and description you put on each page individually, having 60 and 160 characters respectively.

If you use something like %page_title% | %blog_title%, then the title you put on an individual page will be appended with the name of your website at the end.

Finally, these plugins also allow you to mark with a 'Noindex' certain pages, so that they are not indexed by Google, since you may know that you are consciously duplicating content, or that it is an empty page with a single contact form and you don't want people to see that page from Google's results.

3) WPML

If you want to make a web page in different languages, you will need this plugin as it will allow you to edit and duplicate all your content to each language.

It's a paid one ($29 once from https://wpml.org/), but it is very useful and you can use it on all your websites. There are many templates that already include it, so this can be one of your conditions when choosing it.

Among its configurations, you will see that it will allow you to choose how you want to display the pages in their different languages. I always choose directory mode, e.g., /es/, /de/, etc.

Among the options, you will find one of 'Hide languages' which will allow you to be able to translate all the content calmly without having to publish the changes, until you have them all complete.

Now, you only have to edit your page as usual and you will see to the right the other languages with one plus '+' if you have not yet created that language version or a pencil to edit the existing one, both will take you to the same editable page in that language.

I also recommend installing the plugin 'WPML flag in menu' if you want to show the selector flags in your menu, as you can see on my website bernatriera.es.

4) Revolution Slider

There are other simpler solutions to create sliders on your home page and most templates will already include it by default, but Revolution Slider is the one that looks more professional and allows you to do more complex and attractive configurations.

It allows you to display a landscape image with a fade in or zoom in effect superimposed with text (or other images) at different times, giving it a very dynamic and modern effect for your home page.

You could look for a tutorial to understand all the possible configurations you have, but neither are necessary. The sliders that come as examples (if you don't have any, you can download it at:

http://revolution.themepunch.com/example-downloads/) are the best way to learn how to manage them.

Download the one you like the most from this link, import it from its settings and modify text and images to adapt it to your website. You will discover that each slide has its own configuration: time and movement of letters or images, positioning of elements on the screen, transitions, etc.

5) WooCommerce

It is the most essential plugin in WordPress online stores. In fact, it'll probably also be included in your template if you have chosen one for Ecommerce. It allows you to easily create products, accept online payments, set up stock and track sales and revenue.

There are many other plugins that complement this ecommerce plugin that you may be interested in, such as YITH WooCommerce Zoom Magnifier that zooms over the image of the products when you hover over them, or WooCommerce Product Archive Customizer, to change the number of products shown per page.

A complementary plugin that I use a lot is WooCommerce Email Inquiry & Cart Options which allows me to display an individual form in each product, since many users before buying, prefer to make sure that it meets their expectations. When someone completes this form, we will receive an email containing their questions and a link of the product to which they referred.

6) Broken Link Checker

It is one of my favourite ones to detect broken links on your page, meaning, the links from our site that point to a URL and this returns a server error (500) or page not found (404). It is very important not to have broken links in our website since Google penalises us by lowering our SEO positioning.

7) Loco

If you want to make a website in a language other than English, this plugin will be a basic in your list. Many templates and plugins come in English only and with Loco, you can manually translate what you see displayed in English on your page to the right language.

Go to the plugin and choose the package where the line of text you want to translate could be, for example, if it is something from a plugin that you have installed (e.g. WooCommerce), select it and click the language you want to translate. Insert the phrase in the search box and once you find it, add your translation in the respective text box.

8) Duplicator

Duplicator allows you to make a full copy of your website exporting all your web as you see it with all its configurations and data from the database to be imported in another hosting or simply, to another folder in your own hosting.

I use it mainly as a backup to have my site saved while it works, just in case something goes wrong one day. So, while I detect and fix the problem, I want to make sure that my visitors don't go to a 'Server Error 500', so I quickly forward my visitors to my duplicated web, saved in my FTP in another directory, such as /webrestaurant-backup/.

Creating a duplicate is very easy. You only have to follow these steps:

1. Click 'Duplicator' in the vertical menu on the left to access the packages already created and their configuration.
2. Create a new one by selecting 'Create new package' on the right.
3. The 'installer' step is optional and it serves to configure the new URL where the web will be, as well as the details of a new database, if any.
4. You will then check if everything is ready to duplicate the web. You may have some warnings, but as long as you have no errors,

you can complete the process with 'Build', which will generate 2 files, an installer.php and another .zip with all the heavy content. Download them and save them in a folder on your computer for when it is necessary to recover the web.

Now that you have the files, I'll explain what you should do if you want to move your duplicated web to another domain or FTP folder:

5. Create a new database from your hosting control panel, in which you will have to store and install this duplicated site.
6. Access your new web folder through FTP where the new domain will point and upload the two files that you previously downloaded from the duplicator plugin from the original website.
7. Set the new domain to point to that folder, for example: /webrestaurant2/
8. Insert that URL into the browser, followed by /installer.php, for example newrestaurant.com/installer.php and you will be shown a Duplicator installation window requesting the details of the new database, new username and password, which you obtained on the fifth step.
9. Proceed with the installation of your duplicate web and once you have checked that everything went well, you can delete the installation files, as they will only take up space.

9) Contact Form 7

It's the king of plugins for contact forms. Although there are many others, this is the most popular one. It's included in most templates, but if it isn't, you should install it in your WordPress.

It allows you to request all the information you want from your visitors by creating a nice and visual contact form. You can create text fields of different sizes, show different selection options, make some fields mandatory, insert re-captcha among other functions.

In the 'Email' tab, you can define how the email you receive once someone completes the form will be like. You just need to add the fields from the form that you asked i.e. [email] or [name] in this email template, so that email will show you those values inserted.

Finally, for me it is very important to keep the users navigating after completing the form (as it's usually the last step before they leave), so in 'additional settings', I put this line of code which will redirect them to wherever I want, like a thank you page:

```
On_sent_ok:
"location.replace('http://www.mysite.com/thankyou/');"
```

Forwarding users to the new thank you page that I have created, I confirm the receipt of their contact request and take advantage of it to show other services or products that they might be interested in. In addition, you can use that confirmation page to place any conversion codes from other platforms like Google Analytics or AdWords to indicate that an action has been completed, which could be a contact or a sale.

10) XML Sitemap & Google News or Google XML Sitemap

These plugins create automatically the sitemap of your website which is a list of all the different URLs that your website has, along with every page's priority over others on how often its content change, so Google needs to crawl it with more or less frequency.

These two plugins do a similar job, but for me, the biggest difference will depend if your page is multilingual and you are using the plugin WPML mentioned before or not. 'XML Sitemap & Google News' is more complete, although it does not detect the pages in other languages in other directories as /en/, instead, the second (Google XML Sitemap) does.

ADDING WIDGETS: FINAL COMPLEMENTS

Widgets are small pre-defined spaces on your page that allow you to show different functionalities and they are different in each template. The most common positions for widgets in templates are on the sides and on the footer.

You can find them in the vertical menu on the left hand side of your admin WordPress panel, in 'Appearance', 'Widgets'. In this screen, you will see two groups of things:

- On the right, you can see all possible places where there is room for widgets. These can be specified by your template (Home widget, Blog, ...) or more generics (Right column, Footer, ...).

  It is interesting to choose well because, for example, in the publications of your blog, you are more interested in showing the user a list of other publications to continue reading, a category menu or filtering by date of entries., instead of another possibility like your Facebook page news stream.

  In the footer, it is more common to insert a text as a copyright, a menu with the most relevant links, contact information or other small pieces of text like 'about us'.

- On the left, you have all those features that can be added to your widgets on the right. Just select one, drag and drop them wherever you want them.

  Once you have placed a functionality on a widget, it will be displayed with the options or settings they need, i.e. if you show a Facebook add-on to show your Facebook page fans, you must configure it with your Facebook page.

12. SECURITY ON YOUR WORDPRESS

AVOID YOUR BUSINESS BEING COPIED OR BLOCKED

All the technical work is almost done, now you will have to do the most difficult task: create good content and offer great services to your users.

But before that and since you're with your hands on the technical side yet, let me advise you on some small tips on how to protect your page from possible cyber attacks, prevent you from being copied, spam comments or avoid your web to be inaccessible.

It should be noted that all these recommendations are only small obstacles to whoever wants to bother you, but we know that if hackers can have access to US government websites, they will also know how to access yours. Nevertheless, here are some of the best recommendations to protect your WordPress:

Delete install.php y upgrade.php

One of the main security points that are recommended, even in the WordPress website, as a point after the installation of the CMS, is to delete the following files:

- wp-admin/install.php
- wp-admin/upgrade.php

Don't worry, you will not need them anymore.

Extra protection for the config.php file

It is one of the files with more sensitive information. Remember, it is where you put all the information about your database, which would allow anyone to steal all the information in it.

The first thing you should do is to change it from its folder when possible. Now, it is in the root of your /webrestaurant/ folder, but this file can be in an upper level, so for those who look for it in /webrestaurant/config.php, they will no longer find it.

And finally, you can block all modification and reading of the *config.php* file modifying the file *.htaccess*, also from your root folder. Enter these lines at the beginning of the file.

```
<fileswp-config.php>
orderallow,deny
deny from all
</files>
```

Complex passwords for BBDD, FTP and users

If I told you that the basics in online security is to have complex passwords, it's not a new thing, is it? Well, here I will stress that.

The database and FTP access should have very long passwords full of symbols, numbers and lower case and uppercase letters because you will not need them after the initial configuration, so save them in a secure key reminder software or txt doc in case one day you need them, but make sure the robots out there can not easily figure it out.

For users accessing the site, whether administrators, editors, subscribers, etc., make sure that they use strong passwords, even if they will need to be easier than the previous ones as these will be used very often and need to be remembered.

Check your template

There are template developers that could have interests beyond selling templates or plugins, and a classic one is to hide links to their own website to gain popularity in SEO rankings.

There is a plugin that checks the authenticity and purity of the theme or template with a single click: 'TAC Theme'.

Once you have checked it, you can disable the plugin again, but every time you decide to install a new template, make sure you run this scan.

Create backups frequently

I create a monthly backup of all my websites and I rarely have had to use them, but we already know that prevention is better than cure, since if you don't back up, you could lose all your work if one day something goes wrong.

I covered earlier a plugin called Duplicator to fully copy your files and database, but if you are only interested in the database, you can use another plugin called 'UpdraftPlus WordPress Backup'.

Change the user name

70% of users choose 'admin' as the user name of the admins, since it is the one shown by default in WordPress. Be sure to use a name that is harder to guess, and is not the name of the business or domain.

Askimet plugin

This plugin allows you to reduce and filter SPAM comments that you may receive on the web, mostly used by robots to get links back to their websites and improve their position in Google, although at this time this would no longer work for them.

To activate it, you must register first for free on the website and get an API (key to connect your WordPress). Then it's ready to go.

ReCaptcha by Google

The great solution from Google. ReCaptcha reduces abuse and SPAM with a simple check in your forms to distinguish bots from humans.

A verification field will be added in your 'Contact Form 7' before submitting, but first you will need to register your site on Google to get the API keys visiting google.com/recaptcha.

Once registered, go to your contact form plugin menu, 'Integration', and insert your ReCaptcha API keys in there.

13. FAST LANE: LANDING PAGE DEVELOPMENT

A LANDING PAGE TO GENERATE MORE CONVERSIONS

A landing page is where your users will land on your website once they clicked on a link from somewhere else. This traffic could be from different sources, such as search organic results, online advertising, social networks among others.

Landing pages try to capture the attention and focus of the visitor to complete a certain task without distractions, instead of sending them to the main website which offers a better user experience, but lengthens the time and process of conversion and the user may deviate from our primary goal which might be the purchase, fill out the form, request an appointment, or a call to your business: actions that we will name 'conversions' and that how we will measure the success of our online business. Landing pages must have a very clear message or proposition, elaborating about the value of a single product or service.

If you show the landing page to a friend and he or she is not able to identify your goal in 10 seconds, something is wrong. The more specific your landing pages is to the campaign goal, the higher the conversion rate will be.

Normally, they don't get well positioned organically in search engines, because of their lack of content compared to an entire web and being unable to provide a complete user experience. They are not trying to substitute a good web page, but will be used for advertising campaigns where the conversion of new users or sales is key to justify the investment.

They are also much more versatile to modifications, rather than changing your main web, allowing you, for instance, to be present in multiple languages and countries, quickly translating the landing page only or to test different versions using AB testing tools.

BEST PRACTICES CREATING A LANDING PAGE

Here, I present to you the best practices in creating landing pages, although we know that you cannot develop the perfect page for each user, but you will try to optimise it for the majority:

- The choice blocks users and buyers. Try to offer a single option when possible, a unique value proposition with a single action that your client must complete.
- Remove all navigation items you can: the menu, tabs, or different pages to which the user could go before the final action.
- Remove the links from logos or texts to prevent your user from clicking and going to the main web of the company or another domain.
- Offer something different from your main website, so that users see an added value on that page: a limited offer, a promotional code, or a special service.
- Don't save on details about the product they are going to buy: one thing is to simplify the site as much as you can, but another is to eliminate relevant information that users may need and therefore go to look for it elsewhere.
- Respect the brand: Be faithful to your branding on your landing page design, because if not, they may think they went to a doggy page. Make an effort on colours, logos, typography and anything that characterises your company.

TYPES OF LANDING PAGES

Next, I will categorise the possible types of landing pages and some tricks that you should not forget. My favourite is the microsite, but like everything else, it's better to know all the options and decide according to your case and purpose:

One pager

It can be very complete and as long (vertically) as you want. There are examples in which I have seen the use of scrolling down in a very intelligent way showing sequentially how your product or service works and with a final message indicating the next step to finally buy it (your goal).

For example, I landed on this page from Hootsuite after clicking in one of their ads which the only goal for me to try their subscription-based product, but limiting my navigation or research, just right to the point.

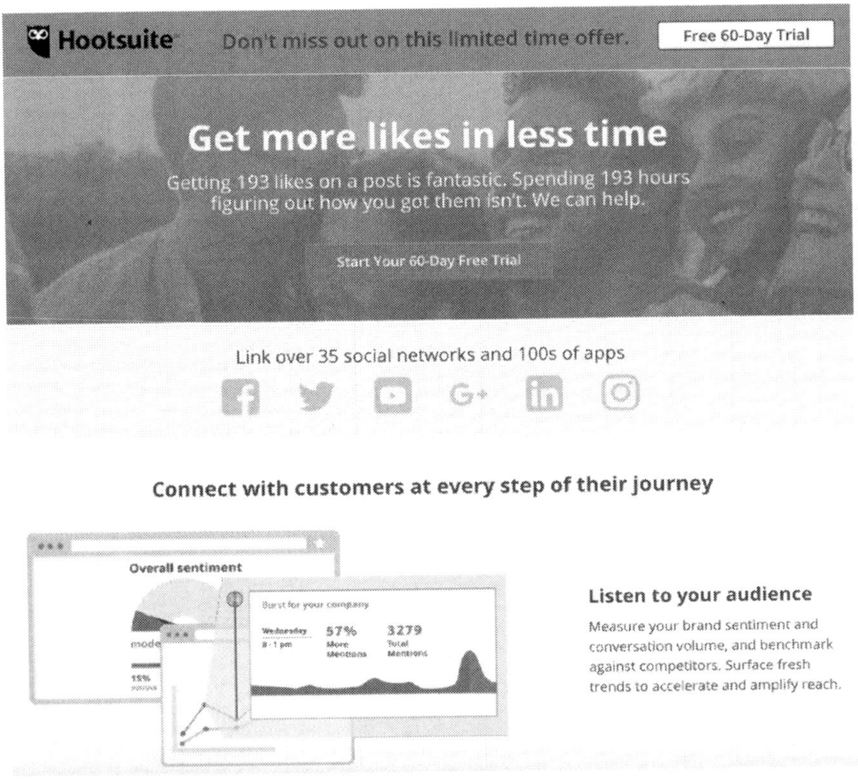

Microsites

These landing pages consist of creating a small web of few pages specifically created for this purpose. You can have a very simple navigation menu linking those few pages that contain different information, but you must make sure that the user does not leave the domain nor click on the logo or any link.

Microsites offer a better user experience than a single landing page and your customers associate it more naturally with your brand and your main web.

Define your target very clearly and keep it in mind on every page of this microsite. For example, if you want to measure number of contacts, you should have a small form present on each page or at least one prominent button inviting to contact.

Microsites are highly recommended when your main web contains too much content, or too many domains (or subdomains) which make it very easy for visitors to get distracted and wanting to cover so much information or deciding to leave it for later. The paradox of choice: the more options, the harder it is to choose one.

Full website

You could be sending the traffic to your main website as long as you are doing a brand campaign to promote awareness and what better destination to showcase your full content than your entire web, full of services and products.

It is also better to send traffic to the web when you want to increase sales in your ecommerce because creating a specific landing page or microsite for each product or category wouldn't be a straight forward solution.

14. CREATE A LANDING PAGE IN 25 MIN WITH INSTAPAGE

In the first chapter, I showed you how to create complete and professional web pages with WordPress, but to launch landing pages, we can use a tool much simpler, intuitive and with a completely professional finish.

Instapage is a web application based on the use of templates and its modification, similar to WordPress, but for a single page and the majority of them already optimised for the generation of conversions through contact forms. In addition, without neglecting the experience of the page in mobile devices because all the templates that are offered are already responsive to any size of screen.

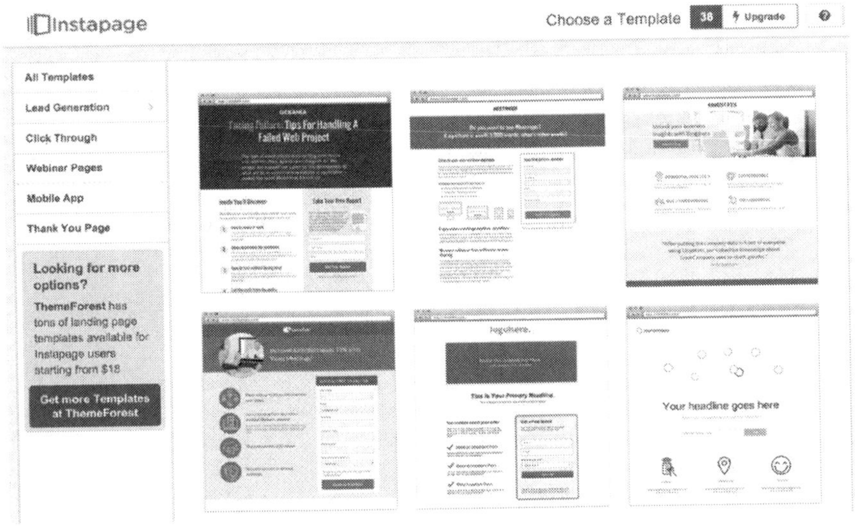

Let's create a landing page in 5 steps:

1. Register and choose a template

Sign up to Instapage.com and create an account in few seconds. Now, you just have to choose a template from the free ones displayed on the web or you can upload another more elaborated and paid from that same portal where we looked at templates for WordPress (themeforest.com). You will find a section named 'landing pages' with a subcategory called Instapage with hundreds of great designs.

Select the template with the structure of content that you like the most and that can reduce to the maximum the number of modifications. Look at the positions of the images, logo, form, text, video etc. Since each template is fully customizable, you can create, move and undo any element you see.

2. Edit and personalise the template

I'm sure you'll catch the trick very fast, since it's a very intuitive editor. Select items (such as a text paragraph) and click to display the edit menu for that item.

You will also see that the mouse cursor changes when you are over the section lines (horizontal divisions of the template), allowing you to reduce or increase white space between sections of the page.

To add a complete new section, you can do so by clicking on the '*Add*' tab above, which also allows you to add other elements like a form, images, videos, a countdown, map or even space to enter HTML code among other functions.

3. Connect your contact form with your CRM system or email sender provider.

Once you have spent some time editing the content, the next important step will be the integration of the form, basic part of your conversion path, with your email management system that allows you to send marketing emails later to the leads you collected.

The best services to capture a list of emails and their later management are MailChimp or CampaignMonitor, although you will be able to find some others.

To integrate the form to the system, just click on it and then edit, 'integrations'.

4. Review and adjust the mobile version.

When you've finished your design for computers, it's time to simulate it also for mobile devices.

Go to the menu by clicking on the top editor where you put 'desktop' and select 'mobile'. It will load all the content in vertical mode and simulate the experience that the users will have in their smartphones, even moving the page with the finger.

From here, in addition to editing each section as before, you can also completely hide sections or objects that are not so relevant in mobile or simply want to do everything a little more visual, simpler and faster, since your users browsing from the mobile are in other conditions.

Things to remember when optimizing your landing page to these devices:

- Most surfing from the mobile are on the move or with a more limited browsing time, as they could be doing other things at the same time, so you have to be much more direct and show only the essentials.

- Many navigate through limited data connections and the download size of the page will influence their navigation, so make it light without large images that slows down their experience.
- The reduced size of the screen is an obvious condition, but many webmasters forget it. Remember that all the images you show will look small, so you want to avoid them containing much detail. The font size should be large enough for you to read easily even moving, but not huge as you will only see few words on the screen and will require a lot of vertical scrolling.

5. Go live through your preferred system

Once you have finished your page and you are ready to push it live, you will have the following options by clicking in the upper right corner 'Publish'. These options are:

- Add it to your WordPress CMS

If this page is going to belong to a larger project, which would be the usual and you have already followed the steps of the previous chapters on creating a page with WordPress, then this option will be a straight forward solution.

You will not have to do anything else than go to your WordPress and download the 'Instapage' plugin and log in through it.

Immediately, you will see there the projects created in your Instapage.com where you can select the one you want to publish, even choosing the URL address in which you want it to be under your own domain.

- Personalised domain

If you choose this option because you don't have a CMS like WordPress or Drupal or because you just prefer to host it in a specific and new domain, then you can choose this option. You will get the DNS domain addresses, which you must configure in your domain provider. Obviously, this requires to own the domain you want in the first place.

- Leave it with the Instapage domain (Demopage)

If you are not very interested to look professional and you are limited in time or money, you always have the option of hosting it in the Instapage domain for free.

15. SHOPIFY AS AN ALTERNATIVE ECOMMERCE

If you have followed all the steps to create a web with WordPress, you have most likely chosen a template that it's an Ecommerce and 90% of E-stores in WordPress brings the built-in plugin WooCommerce, which it's a great Ecommerce plugin that if you don't have it by default, you can also download it and install it in a few seconds.

If you had problems with the purchase or installation of the hosting, domain, downloading and installing WordPress or any other along these processes, firstly let me apologise and I will try to improve the section in the next edition of the book, but secondly, don't worry: we have a plan B, Shopify!

ADVANTAGES OF SHOPIFY

Shopify is a different concept than the website templates we have seen so far. It works as a monthly subscription to use the web application (with different pricing models from $29/mo to $299/mo) that will allow you to have an online store ready to sell in hours.

Here, I list some of its advantages, I am sure you will find it a very valid option:

- You don't need to buy hosting. Shopify is hosted on its own servers, so you save yourself some dollars and other headaches such as configuration of hosting, providers, encryption levels or security on user payments.
- Continuously updated. You will always have the latest version of the software and it is included in the price.
- A lot of templates available to customise design just like WordPress, with very modern designs and responsive to all screens sizes.

- Optimised for SEO. You can edit your titles, descriptions, URLs and other parameters fully customizable for your organic positioning strategy across all your inventory.
- A very fast platform to load, since the resources available from the Shopify servers are much powerful than any of us could have separately.
- Many plugins available to increase the capabilities and features of your store.
- The entire stock management system, secure online payments, reports and delivery systems integrated from the first minute.
- Different options to publish your web or as they call it, distribution through channels. The interesting thing is you can have your store in a domain as a distribution channel, which we took for granted, but Shopify also allows you to sell on your Facebook page, which could be a very interesting solution if you have many followers in your social network.

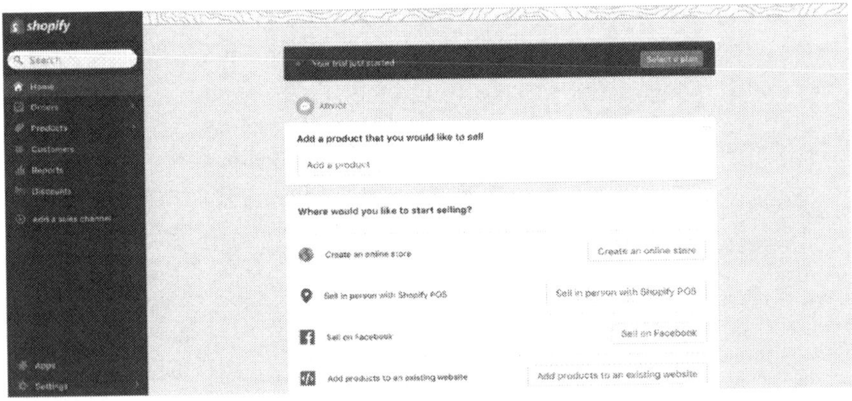

CREATING THE STORE

You can register for free with your trial version to see how easy it is to configure and prepare your stock of products to sell online, although you will not be able to launch the store until you pay the subscription.

You can sign up in two simple steps, introducing your main information and once inside, you can finish setting the most crucial factors for the good operation of the store, such as online payments, taxes or VAT that you want to include on your products, stock, which countries you can deliver to, among many other options.

Start creating your inventory by adding new products, as I show in the following example. You will find a large range of options like to add different features (like colours or sizes of a t-shirt), to duplicate products to simplify your work or to select categories so that the customers filter by product group.

With little practice, you will become a Shopify professional and you will be able to also create reports to see the performance of your store.

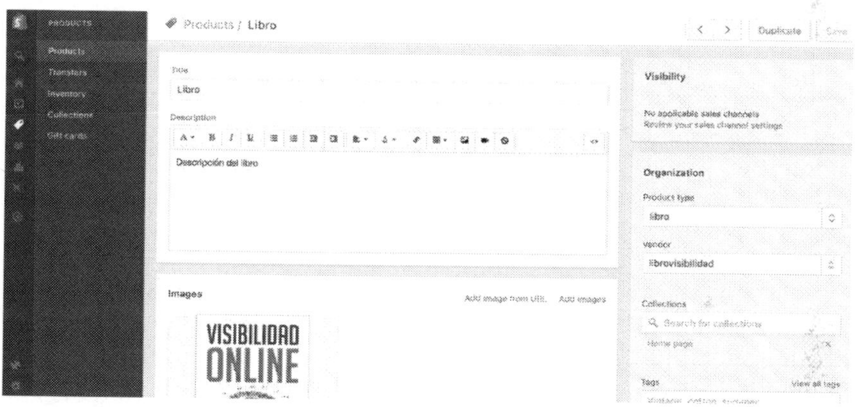

STEP 3

SEO - SEARCH ENGINE OPTIMIZATION ON GOOGLE

16. SEO: FREE VISIBILITY ON GOOGLE

Search Engine Optimization on Google is the process of optimizing your website in order to rank it on the first results after a specific search query. Google fulfils its promise: providing the best results sorted by their relevance for every user.

Optimised results are the first ones to appear after advertisements, which are paid for. These adverts are the main source of income for Google and their placements can be bought, but not the organic results.

As you read this book, you will find many references about Google; but most also apply in other search engines, such as Bing, Yahoo!, Yandex and Baidu.

When we talk about SEO, we talk about opportunities. Showing flowers to someone who wants them, which is the first major step. Then, if your bouquets are the most elaborate or not, it's a different conversation, but you will always be the first choice.

Before your customer sees any other option, he or she will already be buying your flowers, pots and subscribing to your newsletter to get the latest related to your business. (In *Step 5: Usability and User Experience*, we will analyse some tricks to push your customer to buy more and easier in every visit).

From the moment the user searches for something on Google, he becomes a potential customer with an intentional behaviour. He is the one asking for the product, not you trying to sell him something he isn't interested in. Being among those top results on Google is even more important and decisive for the sale than your website's design. There's absolutely no point in having the best website when no one is visiting it.

Also, being on the top position isn't the same as being on second or third. Each lower position exponentially lowers your chances of getting clicks. If your business' website shows up after the fifth position, or even in the next pages (as each page shows only 10 results), your traffic will be near to zero.

Google is so popular for a simple reason: it offers 10 results per search, better than anyone else. And your website can be among those, you just have to convince Google you are one of those good options.

The factors search engines' algorithms take into account are:

- Keywords inserted in the search box and their possible meanings (not just literally, but on their semantics). What is the user looking for?
- User location. Where is the user located?
- Device used to search. Mobile with WIFI, desktop or tablet?
- Previous navigation history. Who is the user?
- Language set up in the browser.
- *Cookies* stored from other websites.
- Emails stored on Gmail.
- Social pages or profiles followed by the user on social networks.
- And many others...

The different search results you have to become familiar with are shown below.

PAID VS ORGANIC RESULTS

The following image shows Google search results and how they are split, giving the first positions to advertisers who pay to be there. In Step 4: Online Advertising, I'll explain all the techniques and strategies, prices and the different features of Google AdWords, so you can also evaluate buying these positions.

You will notice these results have a small green indicator with the word 'ad' when it serves a result paid by a company as advertising. So in this way, Google tries to keep transparency with their users.

There can be 3 or 4 adverts over the organic search results, depending on how popular the search is, and an additional 2 or 3 ads at the end of the page.

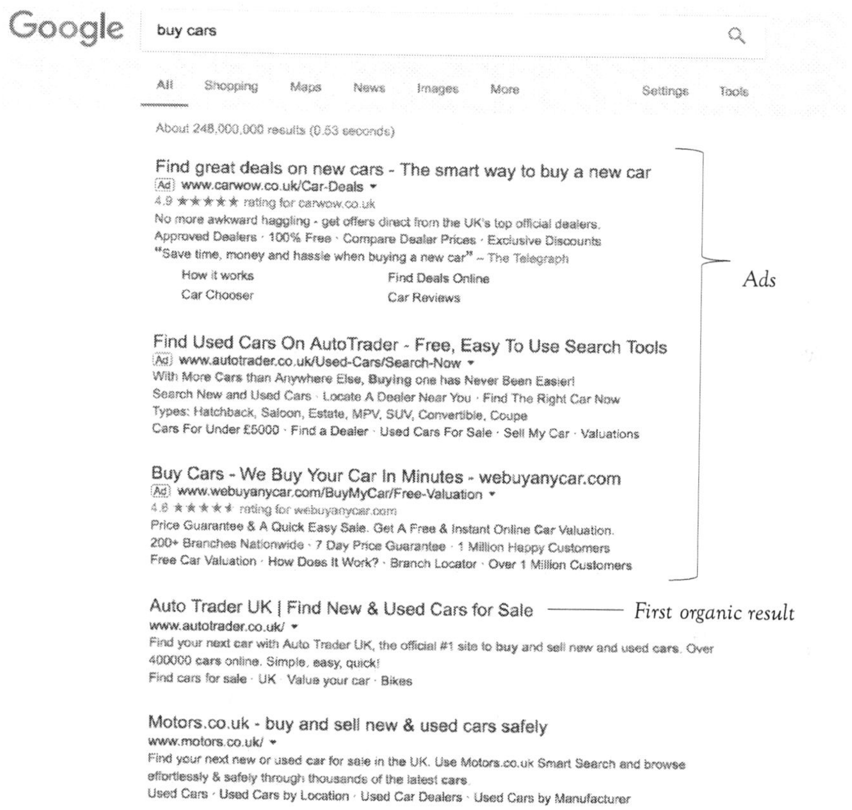

The previous example is very clear. You can't ignore Google's online advertising, which will be covered in *Step 4*. As you can see, even if you put a lot of effort into optimizing your website following SEO techniques, and even making it to the first natural position on Google, you will actually be on the fifth place of its overall list. And if you search using a mobile device, you need to scroll down to read beyond the paid results.

Advertising is the main source of income for Google. However, due to the growing popularity of ad blockers, this income could be at risk. This is why this income strategy has turned more aggressive since 2016, when some changes were made:

- There are no more ads on the right side of the screen. Paid slots are reduced to 4, making them more competitive.
- Ad titles aren't limited to 25 characters anymore. Allowing these to be extended to 60 and make them to look more like SEO results, increasing their click through rate.
- The 'ad' indicator turned green, camouflaging paid results better.

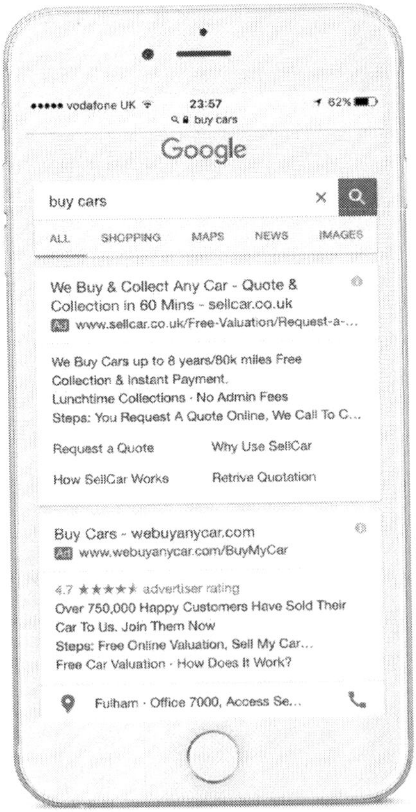

Recent surveys by Google proved that most users don't have an idea of which kind of result they click on. They don't know the difference between an ad and an organic result. This way, they're achieving their goal: users who refused to click ads no longer identify them as such. What does this mean? More money for Google!

But, even with this new scenario, technical optimizations that determine your organic ranking on Google are still very important.

You can still be number 1 for users with an active ad-blocker, you will offer a better website to visitors and benefit when you start running advertising campaigns: the better optimised your website is, the less Google will charge you per click during your advertising campaigns.

We will learn how to optimise the website here, and in Step 6, you will find tools to monitor and analyse how well optimised it is.

17. SEO TECHNIQUES FOR YOUR WEBSITE

Being well ranked on Google means being positioned in your industry against competition that offer similar products and services in the same geographical region.

It is a statistical reality that more users will visit your website than visit your store or physical location. Then, why are so many companies ignoring their online rankings?

Your ranking in Google will determine your visibility, or, as some call it, 'findability'. It is simply about how easy it is for potential customers to find your business.

Next, I will number the most important and easiest SEO optimizations to implement on your website to start improving your ranking compared to your competitions, and of course, some are more important than others.

This is the list of optimizations for your website that I will cover in detail along the section.

- Meta titles and descriptions: Length and messages.
- Headings (h1, h2, h3...) and web structure.
- *robots.txt* and *sitemaps.xml* files.
- URL optimization.
- Webpage loading time.
- Picture and video optimization.
- Creation of unique and relevant content.
- Website localization.
- Bounce rate.
- Responsive and mobile design.
- Link building.

TITLES AND DESCRIPTIONS IN EVERY PAGE

Creating titles and descriptions in your website is a basic step, and also a very important one. This information is shown on Google when your link appears among the results. Title appears in blue and description in black:

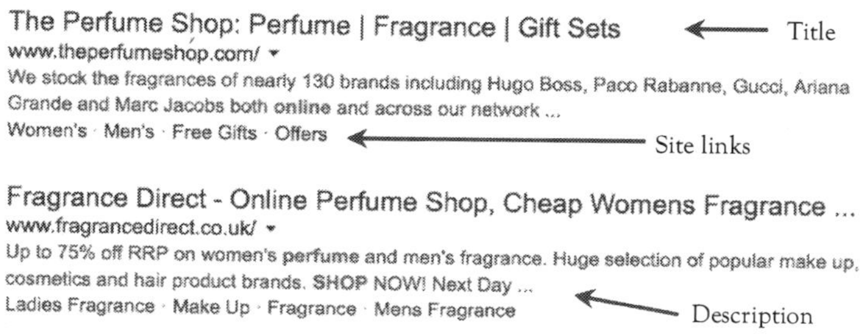

Each page in your website should have a title and a description, including the home page, contact and every product. Basically, everything Google indexes (and tracks) form your site.

These lines will be the first ones users read, even before entering into your store. They are your front door, the ones your customers will see and use as a yardstick in comparing you with your competitions. Why would they click on your result before any other one? You have 3 seconds to convince them with your title.

Ideal titles and descriptions to get the click

Length: If they are too long, Google will shorten them, as shown on the example above from fragancedirect. If there are none or they are too short, they will be generated automatically, based on the content of the pages.

Titles should be shorter than 60 characters or 512 pixels. Descriptions should be less than 160 characters or 920 pixels long.

Google creates a maximum number of pixels, apart from the character limitation, because the same word can occupy different space (or pixels) in the results. To explain the difference, let's see an example with almost identical titles, with the only difference of capitalisation:

Calvin Klein OBSESSED - Buy The New Fragrance From CK (width: 433px)
Calvin Klein obsessed - Buy The New Fragrance From CK (width: 413px)
Calvin Klein obsessed - Buy the new fragrance from CK (width: 395px)

To measure pixels in your titles and descriptions, you can simply use this online tool: http://www.webshoptimizer.com/page-title-pixel-meter/

Messages in your titles and descriptions

Unless you own a famous brand, don't waste characters repeating your name or including your brand. This won't attract anyone.

The most important thing is that you use your title to represent your content in the war of rankings. It's not about the *home page*. Each page can be powerful and allow the user predict its content with its title. If it doesn't, you're lying to them.

If the page is about a sauce recipe, ask yourself the most likely words the users could use to search for it on Google. Afterwards, try to use a combination of those words, as close as you can to start the title with them. Remember Google shows in bold those words from the titles and descriptions that match with the search query.

If you had a page about duck recipes, these could be a bad and good titles:

Bad example:

Duck Recipes : Food Network | Food Network
www.foodnetwork.com/topics/duck ▾
Find **duck** recipes, videos, and ideas from Food Network.

Optimised title:

Duck Recipes - Easy Duck Recipes with Maple Leaf Farms Duck
www.mapleleaffarms.com/duck-recipes ▾
Maple Leaf Farms duck recipes: Find roast duck recipes, crispy duck recipes, duck breast recipes, Christmas duck, confit duck leg recipes, whole duck recipes.

Once you decide a title, use the description to go a bit deeper in details. Always talking about what the users will find on your page. Do this following the same principle, trying to use keywords your users would type as search terms.

To change these parameters on your website, you have to download a plugin for your WordPress, which will allow you to change titles, descriptions and other SEO features in every page easily. Two good options are *All in One SEO* and *Yoast*; both are compatible with different languages if you use them along with WPML.

HEADINGS (H1, H2,...) ON EVERY PAGE AND WEB STRUCTURE

Headings organise your content in-page, creating a hierarchy. They are important because not all the sentences have the same importance, and this will be obvious in your design and the use of HTML tags like H1, H2, H3, H4, H5 and H6.

Imagine a newspaper, the top title would be our heading 1, or H1. Afterwards, you have subtitles, other small bold words, etc. These parts are H2, H3, and so on.

The structure should be pyramidal and logical. The most important heading, H1, should be unique and the only one, so the ideal page should have one H1, some H2, and more H3, up to H6 if there's a lot of content. Avoid having 3 H1's and one H3. That would make no sense for Google's robots.

To convert a title into an H1, you just need to select it on your WordPress editor and click formatting option 'Heading 1'.

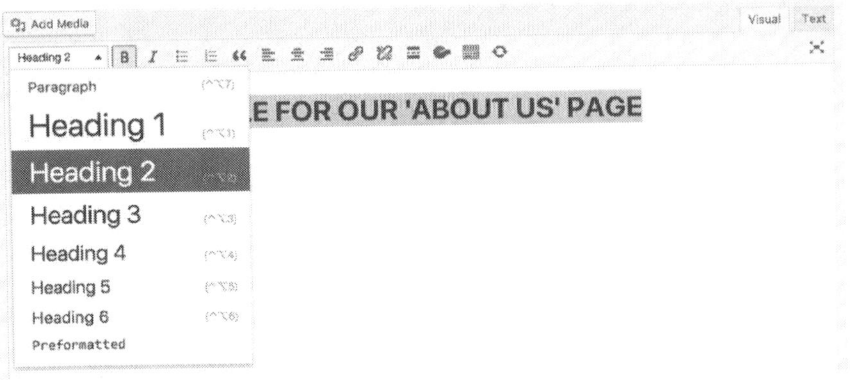

To check any webpage' structure, you can use a Google Chrome extension, such as *Web Developer* or online tools like http://www.seoreviewtools.com/html-headings-checker/

An example of a good heading layout is shown below:

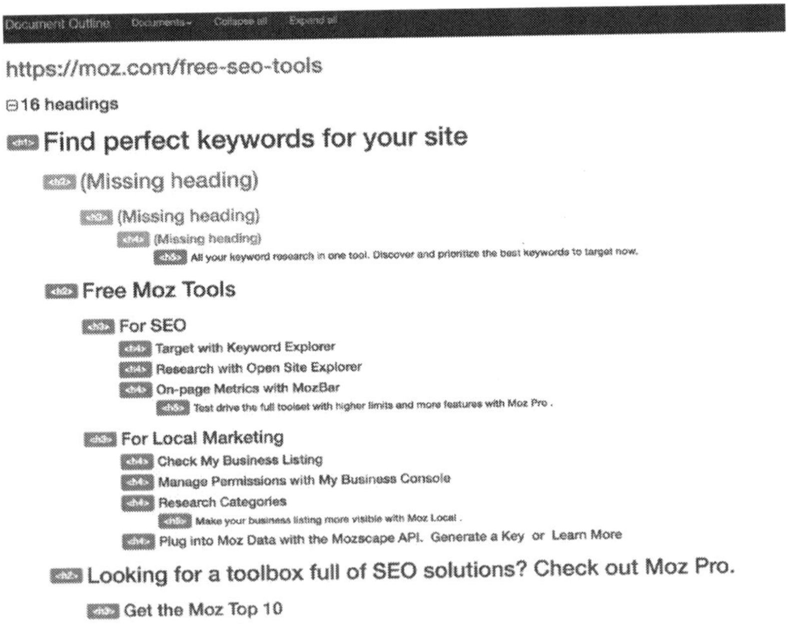

ROBOTS.TXT AND SITEMAP.XML FILES FOR SEARCH ENGINES

When you develop your website, consider including these two files as an essential part of the process. They're easy to create and it's important to know how they work and avoid making mistakes. Both *robots.txt* and *sitemap.xml* are read by every search engine's robots looking for information on what they can and can't scan from your website's architecture (*sitemap*).

Any of the WordPress plugins I mentioned earlier is designed to create these two files automatically, but it is good to know their functions, and how to create and edit them manually when it's needed.

Robots.txt

This file can have very few lines of code and must be hosted on your website's main folder (root domain). For example: mywebsite.com/robots.txt. It's the doorbell that search engines ring to ask for permission to scan your website and to find out what's in it, so they can offer your website among its search results later. We obviously want robots to scan our website, so robots.txt has to reflect that.

To create *robots.txt*, you only have to create a text file (.txt) and add the lines of text you want, which you will learn in the next minute. Save the file with that name, '*robots.txt*', and upload it to your website through FTP (mywebsite.com/robots.txt).

Now, I will show you some examples of a more complex use of this file, authorizing only specific robots (for example, allowing Google and blocking Yahoo!) or giving general access and blocking some folders like wp-admin on which Google shouldn't find anything interesting. Let's have a look.

Simple *robots.txt* that grants full access:

```
User-agent: *
Disallow:          (or Allow: /)
```

'User-agent' parameter identifies what robots are the following instructions for. If it has an asterisk (*) as seen in the example above, it means the instructions apply to all of them.

Allow or Disallow need to be used correctly and they can allow the robots to scan everything if it has this symbol: (/) or nothing: ( ) respectively. As you may be thinking, allowing everything or blocking nothing mean exactly the same thing.

Another example below shows the robots.txt file blocking Bing's access to your folder 'images', except for the logo inside that folder.:

```
User-agent: Bingbot
Disallow: /images/
Allow: /images/logo.png
```

You can also use the asterisk (*) to indicate any combination of names or files like shown next, an example of a robots.txt blocking access to all folders that their names start with wp-, such as wp-admin, wp-content, and wp-includes:

```
User-agent: *
Disallow: /wp-*/
```

The same can be done with all files of the same type. For example, PDF:

```
Disallow: *.pdf
```

Or subfolders stored in the same location, no matter their name:

```
Disallow: /wp-content/uploads/*/*/holiday*.jpg
```

Finally, you can also use robots.txt to show Google where to find the sitemap.xml (which will be explained next)

```
Sitemap: http://www.miweb.com/sitemap.xml
```

Sitemap.xml

Once the search engine knocks the door and robots.txt authorises its entrance, sitemap.xml would be like the menu of a restaurant. Sitemap contains a list with all different URLs or web pages, each with a specific priority percentage expressed with values between 0 and 1, along with a guide on how often its content is updated.

This XML file does not appear to have any style information associated with it. The document tree is shown below.


```
▼<urlset xmlns="http://www.sitemaps.org/schemas/sitemap/0.9">
  ▼<url>
     <loc>https://moz.com/blog/basic-local-competitive-audit</loc>
     <lastmod>2017-08-22</lastmod>
   </url>
  ▼<url>
     <loc>https://moz.com/blog/enterprise-seo-efficacy</loc>
     <lastmod>2017-08-22</lastmod>
   </url>
  ▼<url>
    ▼<loc>
       https://moz.com/blog/lessons-from-failed-link-building
     </loc>
     <lastmod>2017-08-22</lastmod>
   </url>
  ▼<url>
     <loc>https://moz.com/blog/earn-links-directly</loc>
     <lastmod>2017-08-22</lastmod>
   </url>
  ▼<url>
    ▼<loc>
       https://moz.com/blog/find-competitor-backlinks-next-level
     </loc>
     <lastmod>2017-08-22</lastmod>
   </url>
  ▼<url>
     <loc>https://moz.com/blog/organic-quality-score</loc>
     <lastmod>2017-08-22</lastmod>
   </url>
  ▼<url>
     <loc>https://moz.com/blog/seo-above-the-funnel</loc>
     <lastmod>2017-08-22</lastmod>
   </url>
  ▼<url>
     <loc>https://moz.com/blog/roi-local-seo</loc>
     <lastmod>2017-08-22</lastmod>
   </url>
```


OPTIMISED USE OF URLS FOR YOUR WEB PAGES

WordPress allows you to edit each page's online address, its URL. By default, an automatic URL is assigned according to each page's title. If you wish to change this URL or it doesn't fit the best standards (you will learn more about this in the next pages), you can change it.

You will find the page's address under its title, along with an *Edit* button, so you can change the words if necessary.

As you can see, URL structure is very important. It should be related to the main site structure and website's navigation, aiming to include more relevant words in the address.

In this case, I'm helping this 'logos' page to be ranked among *logo* related searches, but also in some other related to website design, as this page belongs under that hierarchy and URL path.

Avoid long addresses, delete prepositions as well as any symbol or number that don't add value to the URL. Try to keep unique URLs using synonyms and other keywords that you think users might type on their searches queries.

REDUCING YOUR WEBSITE LOADING TIME

There's no need to explain how important it is to have a website that loads quickly. Nowadays, we barely have any time to navigate, so evaluation and comparison between websites is measured in milliseconds.

Once users click, you can't make them wait more than a couple seconds to show them your full website. When they navigate through it and looking at different products, each extra second they wait for the page to load will be used in determining if they should be patient or leave.

Loading times are even more important when users navigate from their mobile devices. They're probably on the move, so time allowed to browse and their patience will be even lower than some others sitting in front of a computer.

Different statistical studies proved that every extra 1 second of loading time of your website means 7% less conversion rate, which is directly related to less sales.

How long does your website take to load?

The first thing you have to do is to measure your website's loading time. There are several free tools to do so. One of them is Pingdom tools: http://tools.pingdom.com/fpt/

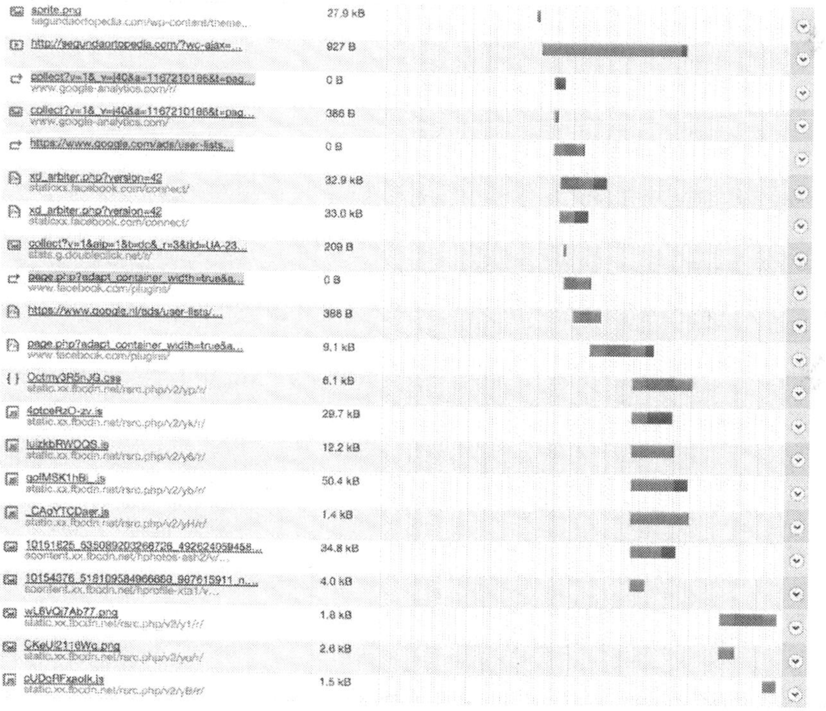

The tool can identify which elements on your website take the longest time to load. For example, you'll learn whether your images are too heavy and need to be optimised, or if your latest plugin is taking too long to load.

Google Page Speed is another great tool to test your loading time with similar features:
https://developers.google.com/speed/pagespeed/insights/

This tool differentiates the test from mobile devices and desktop computers. This gives you a clue about how important the loading times on mobile devices are for Google to define their organic rankings.

Google page speed guides you, but instead of showing a breakdown of every element from your website, it groups them and gives you recommendations based on those. For example: "lower image file size to load this page 35% faster".

The best techniques to improve loading times

1. Dedicated servers for your website

One of the most common mistakes when creating a website is choosing the cheapest hosting packages in the market for your web. Actually, I'm going to reveal my best two decisions while I was learning how to develop optimised websites: "I'm going to try WordPress" and "I will invest more on my hosting".

I already stated at the beginning of the second step the differences between shared and dedicated hosting and discussed RAM memory features. To simplify and avoid repeating myself: the price you pay for a hosting will directly improve your web loading times. If you're not going to get thousands of visits per day, you don't need an expensive one. But, please, don't choose the cheapest one either.

It is also important to have a server with an IP located in the same country where most of your visits come from. I used a server for my local sport facilities website in which my users from the same town than the centre had to travel digitally to the server in Germany before entering to the website. It doesn't make sense, does it?

2. Using a CDN for content distribution

CDN (*Content Delivery Network*) means storing your website content in the 'cloud' of many countries. This way, you allow users to access your content a lot faster and from different geographical locations. You don't force all your traffic to go to the same IP address from a specific country. This isn't an alternative to the server you got, it is just a complement.

You may have noticed during your hosting research that some include a CDN. If they didn't, you can create a free account in one of the most well known CDN providers, such as CloudFare.com. However, their features vary depending on your payment plan.

It is important to remember that any data stored in the cloud is very similar to the website stored in cache, they have the same problems and inconveniences. For instance, when you update the content of your website, it can take longer for the change to be effective for the users. To decrease this delay, all CDNs have a 'development' mode, which allows you to work on the web and send all the updated content back to the cloud.

3. Cache your website and compress its content

One of the main characteristics to lower loading times on your website is preloading the content in the cache memory. You can do this through a plugin I mentioned in the WordPress section, the W3C Cache. This preload will work automatically, like GZIP compression, which reduces your website' size and helps to make downloads lighter.

IMAGES OPTIMIZATION

Images are common elements in a website and they can remarkably change its total size and loading time. Deficient image optimization can multiply by 5 a page' size, without even offering a better quality resolution for users' eyes.

There are several professional tools to help you edit images. A famous one is Photoshop, but you can also use its free version, Gimp, or any other easier alternatives, such as PicMonkey.com.

Lower pixel sizes

Images don't have to be thousands of pixels of width and height when your website will only be shown in computer screens, mobile phones or tablets.

The first thing you should do is to decide where in your website the image will be placed and know the height x width ratio of that placement. I use a Google Chrome extension called Page Ruler that allows me to use a ruler on the screen with my mouse, and get an accurate measurement of the selected area.

Website images shouldn't be more than 2000px long, and I'm talking about big images for photo galleries designed for big monitors. In fact, even if you load a 2000px long image, you will most probably end up showing a version of around 900px, although if the website allows to zoom the image, then a larger one is worth it.

You can be more flexible with image height, because in some cases, a very long image can be seen while scrolling down on your website. If the images are for small illustrations, icons or buttons, then you need to adjust the images to that smaller size.

Image compression and formats

Once it's time to save the edited image, you need to decide something important that could harm your image optimizations: its format or file extension. We want to save the image with the lowest size possible (measured in bytes) without losing visual quality.

- JPG

The most commonly used format is JPG (or JPEG), which mixes different coloured pixels we can't recognise or differentiate with our eyes, reducing the image size.

This format offers several levels of compression and every software you use will ask how much you want to compress the image in JPG and will also offer you a preview, so you can verify how the image changes with compression.

I like to zoom in and see a small detail in the image. Then, I lower quality until changes on that detail are noticeable. This way, I ensure that when I zoom out, the human eye won't notice my compression.

- PNG

One of the most common formats used online. Its advantage is having a transparent background. Very useful in many cases like icons or logos.

If you use Photoshop, there's an option below 'Save as...' called 'Save for web'. This opens a dialogue box where you can choose a PNG configuration. I recommend PNG-24.

Filenames

Although search engines are in constant development, improving their processing and image recognition, it is recommended to help Google to know what our images show. You only need to write some parameters. Remember robots read words easier than any visual message.

So, before uploading your image to the server or through WordPress, make sure it has an appropriate filename that refers to what the website is about. I also recommend deleting special characters, such as accents or dieresis. The browser would have to modify these characters using ASCII. For example, 'á' would turn into: '%&1SS2a'. Also, filenames shouldn't be more than 3 words long, leaving space or hyphens between them.

Examples of good filenames:

`Shirt-nike-red.jpg`

Example of a bad filename:

```
DSC0030.jpg
```

Titles and descriptions

Once you upload your image, you should give it a title and description. These shouldn't be as long as titles and page descriptions are, but they should be able to fulfil a different function.

The title could be the brand or product name of what you are showing, followed by other differential details. Titles are more important than descriptions, which could even be dispensable.

ALT Attribute

One of the most commonly ignored and paradoxically important fields for Google is the ALT attribute. This explains to users (and Google) what is contained in an image, like a friend telling you: "red Nike t-shirt for sale $35".

The ALT attribute is very important for visually impaired and handicapped people. This is why it is very recommended to use it and Google also rewards it, ranking you higher.

VIDEO OPTIMIZATION

If you are going to integrate video into your website, whether they're directly uploaded to your website or linked from external sources like YouTube or Vimeo, always try to keep all related information like you would do with images, and for the same reasons: Google handles better what it can read in words.

The difference with images is that videos create a longer experience. This is why it is recommended that you control video interaction flow and their links to other videos, such as playlists. Keep in mind that after the video ends, an undesired video could play in your website automatically.

Extra tip: Host your videos on YouTube or Vimeo

Insert your video from YouTube or Vimeo and let them host it on their powerful servers. If you upload a video directly to your server, the file could be too big and would slow your loading times.

Integrating a video to your website is like having a window (frame) and showing YouTube's content through it, but the video wouldn't actually be in your website.

To do this, you need a YouTube channel where you can upload all your company's videos. Keep the channel visually attractive with a good heading 2560 x 1140px image and a well written description, up to 1000 characters long, that invites people to act and watch or include links to your site.

If you have a lot of videos, create playlists. Group videos by categories so your users can play them consecutively.

When you upload a video to YouTube, rename the file with relevant words, like you did with images. Add a 5-word title and a description that includes a good summary using keywords for YouTube, which, after all, is the second most widely used search engine, after Google.

Assign your video to several different YouTube categories, and, if you can, write and upload text with your video as subtitles. This way, users can mute the video and still watch and get your message.

You can also add annotations along your video, which could be titles, notes and web cards, suggesting a link for the user to keep flowing through the next video or action. Be careful: if you don't use it appropriately, you will end up distracting users.

PAGE CONTENT OPTIMIZATION

Keywords

One of the most commonly used expressions in marketing online, for both organic rankings and other paid media, might be 'keywords'.

On SEO, keywords had different importance years ago. At the beginning, to get a good organic ranking, you only had to saturate titles, headings, and content with keywords. This meant we would often end up navigating websites made for robots instead of people. Some words and phrases repeated without making any sense.

Since then, Google has improved a lot. Today, it demands that developers and businesses endeavour to write in a natural coherent way for their visitors. In fact, its algorithm can punish a website for overusing keywords. Just use them in phrases and long tail, coherent phrases as naturally as possible.

Each page is a complete and individual world, so your keywords should reflect this uniqueness. If you want to rank as a restaurant in London, set your strategy for the full website, defining its page structure and the goal that every single page has, then optimise and tailor the content of that page with that goal in mind.

If your objective is to rank your website for searches like "restaurant in downtown NYC", then your focus throughout your website, and, most importantly, on your home page, should be relevant to that search.

Although if your restaurant offers live music evenings, then you should dedicate a page for those events and focus the content around that. The food menu shouldn't matter in this case. The goal for this specific page from your website should be to rank for "live jazz music in Manhattan". This way, you'll create relevant pages for specific themes and benefit your overall website ranking.

It is important that, even if I mentioned that you shouldn't overload your site repeating keywords throughout your content (3 or 4 times is more than enough), they should be well distributed. Make sure to include relevant words in:

- The title of the page.

- Description (using synonyms or similar semantic meaning where possible).
- H1 or H2 when words are in a good context and followed by further details in their paragraphs.
- Text: Once or twice in the content is enough.
- Images or videos: if your website has images or videos, it is important to add relevant phrases in your ALT parameter, as I explained before.
- Links: Select other pages other than the one you are optimizing and find relevant text that could be linking to the page. Remember links also have a *title* parameter to help users know what they will find after clicking the link. This small label will be shown when the mouse moves over the link.

Duplicated content

It should be clear by now that Google rewards relevant content by showing them in its first results. But, aside from being relevant, it must be unique.

Imagine Google's first search result is a very relevant one to your query. Now, imagine someone copies this page. Using the same algorithm, should Google show you the copied version on top as well as the original?

Google's algorithm aims to provide the 10 best results on its first page. If two are identical, it would be offering only 9. It is something we would expect Google to have it fixed, and of course, it is.

Duplicated content won't appear on Google. Even if it has been slightly modified, it won't appear near the original on the search results for any search. So you should be careful about two things:

- Don't copy: It is very hard to write content, I understand that, but don't fall in the trap and copy content from your competitors or from some other sources of information. For a while, you may achieve your objective, but on the long run, no one will find your website for the reasons I just mentioned.

- Be vigilant about not being copied: It is bad to copy, but it is also bad to be copied. Also, it's definitely out of your control because your content is public, but you should periodically check that no one else is sharing your text and images. There's a very powerful tool (copyscape.com) that will help you to find out after inserting your URL if the content is duplicated somewhere else.

If your original content was duplicated, there are several things you can do:

- Leave a note to Google, explaining that your content was copied and you own the copyrights for it. You can alert the search engine through this link: *https://support.google.com/legal/answer/1120734*
- Find the webmaster of the website or contact information of the business and send them an email. Inform them they are using your content without permission and warn them you will take legal action if it isn't eliminated within 5 working days.

  Any business owner will want to avoid trouble. Also, it is possible they were not even aware as it was done by their webmaster.

Fresh, updated and sexy content

One of the increasingly more important factors, once all basic SEO techniques are covered, will be the frequent creation of relevant and attractive contents, so users can interact, read and share. This will exponentially increase your free traffic.

Blogs are website sections where content creation is natural and periodic. Because of it, users might follow you on social networks or regularly visit your web to discover your most recent posts.

Key tips to create attractive content that will be shared from person to person:

- Social value

  We share things to look good, either because we are the first to do it or because we want to show our participation in something. Make sure your content adds that social value to users, so they feel the need to share.

  Does talking about your brand make them look good?

- Emotions

  Sharing contents that arouse emotions play an important role in helping us connect with one another. The positive emotions that we share the most are admiration, humour and excitement. On the flip side, the most shared negative emotions are anger and anxiety. Other contents, sweet, nice or sad, aren't really shared.

  Does talking about your brand bring any emotion to them?

- Practical value

  Another reason people share is because they can help or inform about a solution. If they can find usefulness in a piece of your content or brand, they will tell about their finding to someone else. If it's free, of course.

  If you think this book has good tips to help your friend's business to be more visible, wouldn't you recommend it?

- Public

  People like to imitate what others do. Yes, it sounds like an animal instinct, but it works. There are so many alternatives for each solution, but you regularly choose the one chosen by most people, as in the same way you want most people to choose your product or solution.

  When developing a brand or product, make sure it's visible and people see it when your customers use it, easy enough to be identified so it advertises itself.

Don't just translate, but localise

The more relevant your website becomes for a specific location; the more opportunities it will have to rank up on Google on those local searches. Localisation includes several factors you should keep in mind when designing and optimizing your page and creating content:

- Language

The most obvious one, but most business owners forget to have their website on several official and relevant languages for their potential customers and visitors. For example, if your website is published in the United States, your British English should be adapted. If you're working in Switzerland, German, French and Italian languages should be available.

When you have several languages on your website, make sure to let Google know the domains or directories for each language. It can be done very easily using some lines of code called *hreflang*. These are located next to your web's head tags, *<head>* and *</head>*.

For instance, imagine a website with languages in Spanish and English. The English version has no subdomain. The Spanish version has a es. subdomain. These are the lines you should insert in your head tags for Google to know which page to show to its users:

```
<link rel="alternate" hreflang="es-ES"
href="http://es.mywebsite.com/" />

<link rel="alternate" hreflang="en-GB"
href="http://mywebsite.com/" />
```

- Localised relevant keywords

If you own a physical business in a certain city, your content optimization should relate that city with your product or service. This correlation is key for your *online* and *offline* success. You don't want to compete with the whole country. If your company is located in Manhattan, your SEO optimization in titles, content, and links should reflect that. For example: "Lawyers in Manhattan". Or even more specific: "Specialised criminal lawyers in Manhattan".

REGISTER YOUR BUSINESS ON GOOGLE MYBUSINESS

When we search a flower shop, we don't just want it to be in our city, but also near us. Especially if we're searching from our mobile phone. Many searches are done directly in Google Maps. Your presence there, with a good pinpoint and accurate telephone numbers, opening times, addresses, and images, will be crucial to capture new opportunities and potential customers.

One of the most important and popular digital spaces for physical businesses is Google MyBusiness, previously known as Google Places, which acts like a simple business page on your Google+ and will be displayed not only on Google Maps, but also in Google search. When someone searches for your brand, Google will show your main page as one of the results, including logo, map, and some pictures.

Look at how this small and local business is shown on Google when someone searched for the brand, 'CREIX'. All results above the fold are dominated by it, including the business card on the right hand side we created displaying the logo, map, reviews and other very useful information.

Steps to create your Google+ Business page and get total visibility on Google for your brand:

1. Go to https://www.google.es/intx/es_es/business/ and sign in. If you don't have a Google+ account, you will need to sign up first with probably the same Gmail address that you are already using with all the rest of Google products.
2. Add your business telephone number, opening and closing times, your website URL and your address. You should verify your address and telephone through an automatic call and a letter that Google will post to your business address. This

contains a PIN number that once inserted back in the system, Google will show your business as a legit and verified one.

3. Upload your logo, pictures of your business taken from outside and inside, pictures from your products, etc.
4. Specify additional amenities, services or features, like if your business has a car parking, price range of your products, etc.

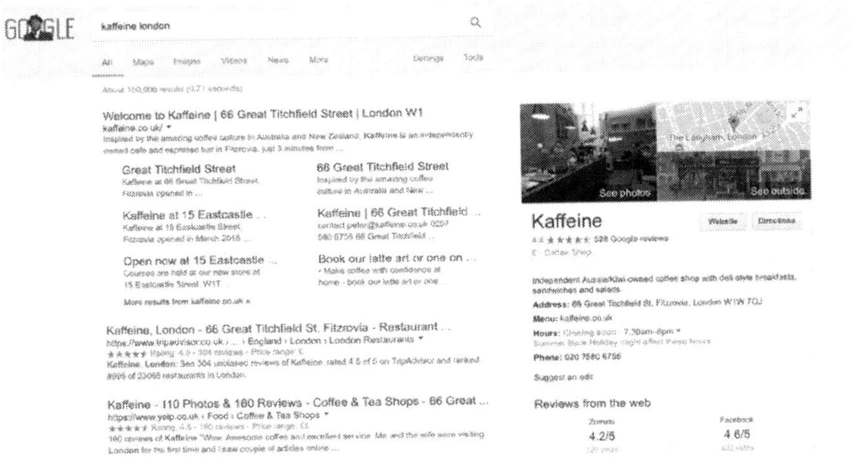

REDUCING YOUR PAGE'S BOUNCE RATE

The bounce rate is one of the more important measurements of your page's efficiency; both in providing a good experience for your users and for Google's evaluations.

This percentage represents the ratio of users that land on your website, but immediately go back to the search results or close the browser tab. This ratio tells Google, and to us, that the result offered was not a good one or at least for that specific user in a given time and place. The bounce rate of every page can be found with Google Analytics (read more about in Step 6).

To reduce your bounce rate, it is very important to be mindful of the words you are optimizing your website with. If you aim to be relevant for golfers in Florida, apart from optimizing your words for that audience, you also need to offer relevant content for them. Users searching for "golf in Florida" could also be thinking about "buy golf sticks", "directory of golf courses", and many others. If your website is just an online store of golf equipment, your strategy should be around that option. Otherwise, users interested in other golf areas may land on your website, but leave shortly. This action will raise your bounce rate, and Google will lower your ranking for the same or similar searches.

To lower this ratio, you have to make sure any user who clicks on your site keeps navigating through it, visiting other pages or spend some time reading them. The number of pages visited and time spent on them is very important for search engines to understand your website offered good content in response to a specific search.

Optimizing your usability and improving the overall user experience are also very important factors for SEO. Despite what other technical SEO and UX professional say, these two areas are intimately intertwined. We will learn more about how we can reduce the bounce rate in Step 5 (UX).

OPTIMIZING FOR MOBILE

Your website has to be optimised for mobile. If you have followed my steps about choosing a WordPress template to build your site, then you are already in a good place with this SEO optimization as most of the templates are already responsive.

It's not hard to guess that Google searches from mobiles increase every month; and Google gives special importance to these: it shows different results, depending on which device you are using to search and where it is.

In fact, on April 22, 2015, Google modified its algorithm to push down websites that weren't optimised for mobile. This created a strong impact on big brands whose adaptations were slower than start-ups. They thought their authority as brands was enough for Google to rank them, but it wasn't.

Your website's design has to adapt to any screen size, and, thinking about mobile, to the smallest ones as well. Your design on mobile should allow an easy read, touch, and navigate with a finger, not two to constantly zoom in.

Use a big font for the text, icons, reduced menus, and telephones numbers you can tap to call straight away. These are some of the best practices on mobile design, and there are many more, but here, I focus only on the ones that can affect your organic ranking. Remember, what matters is that Google recognises your website as mobile optimised. To check what the most important search engine thinks, click and use this testing tool: https://www.google.com/webmasters/tools/mobile-friendly/

LINK BUILDING

This is one of the actions or features with the most potential. It can affect your ranking, positively or negatively.

Links leading to your website from others means they 'endorse' you. But Google's perception on who does it can change everything. Imagine these scenarios:

- Your mother says: "Son, you should visit this bar! It is very cool!"
- Your friend says: "Hey, you should visit this bar! It is very cool!"
- A sommelier and Michelin guide judge says: "Hello, you should visit this bar. I recommend it".
- A complete stranger says: "Hey, would you like to visit this bar? It's very cool!"
- A weird looking guy with a confusing way of speaking says: "Hey, go to this bar, it's very cool..."

They all basically said the same thing, but your opinion about the bar changed based on who said that. You have a perception of the bar. You think you may not like the bar your mother likes. You trust what your friend said. You believe the Michelin judge for his reputation and capacity to compare bars, but maybe his recommendation doesn't fit your budget. You ignore the one you don't know and will be sure to avoid the one mentioned by the last person.

Google understands this mind process and applies it to its algorithms. If there are websites out there linking to yours, it's very beneficial to your ranking because it means people talk about you. And in addition, it will bring more visits to your site. But if the site that links you is a bit doggy, poor content and with a lot of other links, it can have negative consequences to your SEO rankings.

The content where the link is must be relevant to your site. And both websites should be in the same language, so the users can flow smoothly from one another, which is what Google wants.

The more relevant the content and prestige of the websites are, the more the authority that will pass to your website: it isn't the same to have a link that comes from a blog no one reads as being mentioned on a popular online news website (i.e. wsj.com). These links are obviously hard to get.

How to get links from other websites

The best way to get linked is if that happens naturally. This means turning your website into a source of unique and relevant content, so other web owners or businesses feel they should share it with their visitors.

It is important that you avoid paying or exchanging links. When your website gets a certain number of visits, companies with poor credibility will start sending emails talking about SEO and inviting you to exchange links with them: you link their web and they link yours.

A good option to get links to you is to find blogs or sites from your industry and that may contain a page with suggested links to other pages.

Google provides ways to do advanced searches that will help you. Find different combinations here: https://www.google.es/advanced_search. This way, you will find blogs about your industry, but have keywords such as 'Links', 'Guest Blogs', etc.

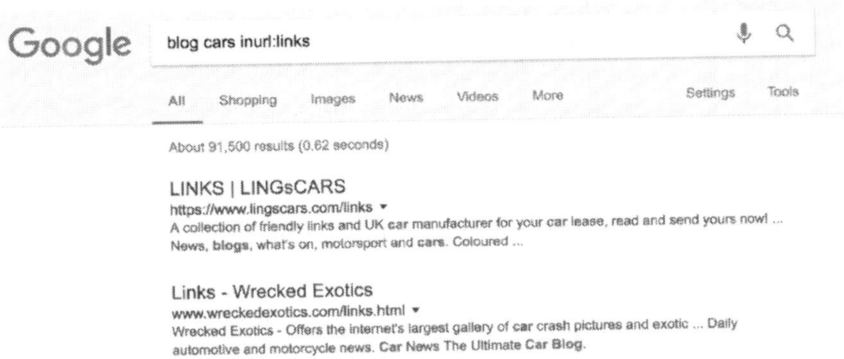

You can also find profiles of relevant people in your industry, with influence over many followers (a.k.a. influencers). If they recommend you, it could be important for your reputation. Register and try this tool for free from MOZ.com: https://moz.com/followerwonk/ and you can search Twitter or Facebook profiles that talk about specific keywords and then sorted by followers.

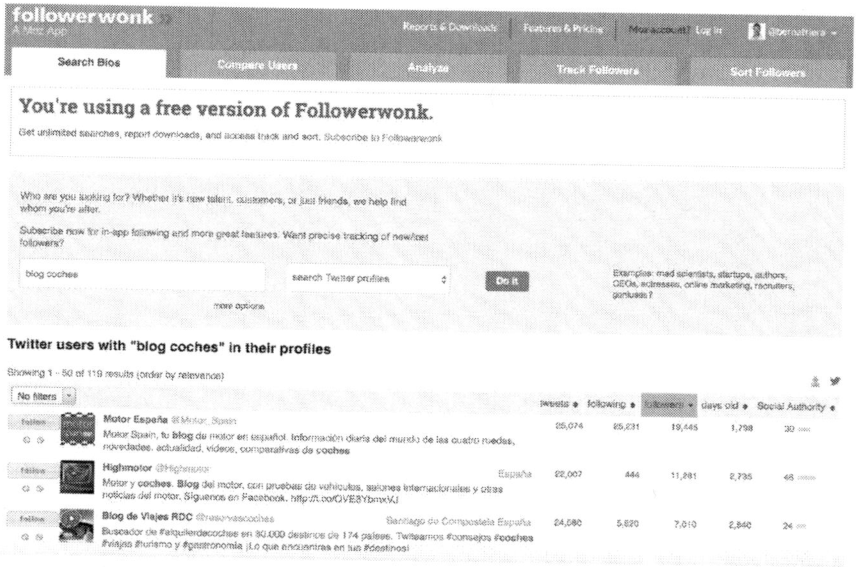
followerwonk
Search Bios
Compare Users
Analyze
Track Followers
Sort Followers
You're using a free version of Followerwonk.
blog coches
search Twitter profiles
Do it
Twitter users with "blog coches" in their profiles
No filters
following
days old
Social Authority
Motor España
Highmotor
Blog de Viajes RDC

18. EXTRA SEO TRICKS FOR ECOMMERCE

After all that's been mentioned to optimise websites and make them visible in Google, now, I will share some additional tricks specifically for your online store.

Sold items are good!

Don't delete sold items. They have been ranking on Google for some time. Deleting them will cause a 404 error and disappear. If you run out of stock, try to indicate that it has been sold out, but keep it accessible. This way, your store will hold one more result on Google and it will keep generating visits. The goal is that customers that arrive to your sold-out product will continue navigating and buying similar products.

Avoid content duplication

Make sure to tell Google Search Console and WordPress not to index your products when they get filtered. Your product can be on several different categories (/used-cars/ and /sport-cars/) and appear as a result of different filters (/red-cars/?filter=red). This is something Google can interpret as page duplication. To explain to Google how you want these parameters to be analysed, go to Google Search Console / Crawl / URL parameters / Add parameter, and define what should be ignored.

Teach Google about the structure of your product pages

Add your products as structured data on Google Search Console. This way, you can ease tracking and indexing for Google among the same type of product pages. I'm talking about those that have a product, prices, SKU, images, among other elements and every product always has the same elements in the same placements.

To mark up content, go to *Search Appearance, Data Highlighter* and *Start Highlighting*. Afterwards, add your product's URL. It will be used as example for other pages with a similar structure. On this following example from DirectSports (also now known as cheapbats.com) they show to Google where reviews are placed, price, title, SKU, etc, so the search engine may provide one of these parameters (like the price or reviews) when users search for “2016 demarini sf8 bat”.

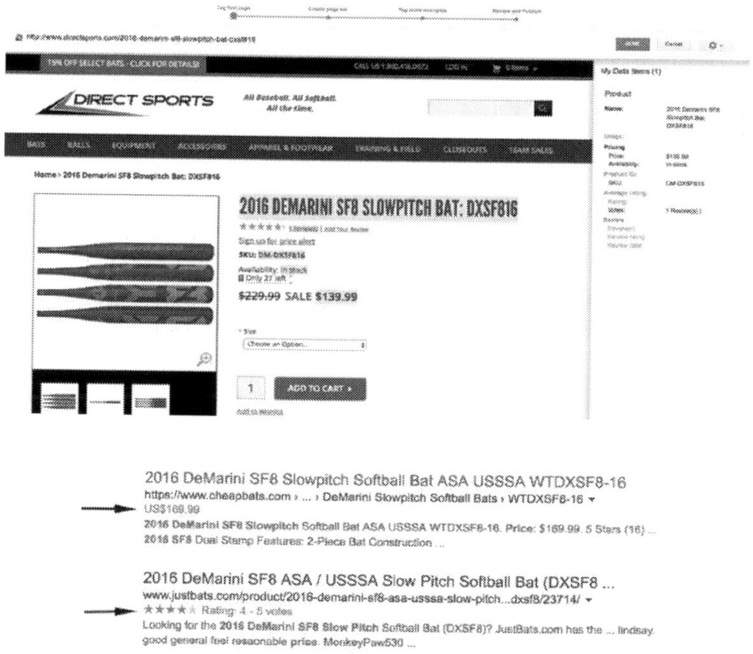

When the page loads, on the right, you will find the data labels that Google expects you to highlight: product name, price, identifier, image, reviews, review authors, among others.

To highlight these labels into your page, you only need to move your mouse to the left where your product page is and click the element. For example, click on the product's price. A dropdown menu with all the options will appear for you to indicate that element is the 'price'.

Once you highlight all the information and you know these will repeat for all your products, click ‘next’. The process will repeat several times with other products until Google understands the pattern and can repeat it automatically.

19. UPDATING YOUR SITE WITHOUT IMPACTING ITS SEO

If you redesigned your whole website, changing its structure and navigation, update content or any other action that may impact the content that is already indexed by Google, could lose all your ranking history on the search engines. To avoid this, make sure to follow these next steps, specific to your case:

You are only updating the content of the page

In this case, search engine's impact will be minimal, if there's any at all. In fact, you should update your content frequently to keep providing fresh material to your users. So don't worry, far from harming you, this change could improve your ranking.

Just keep in mind if the page you want to update links to other pages from your current content, try to keep the links afterwards too.

You are changing permanent links / URLs

The most critical change is the one involving paths or URLs. Remember these are the doors that Google already knows as they have already been indexed. If you change that, Google won't find anything there. Additionally, users trying to access the old URL will get a 404 error (page not found). Google will detect something's wrong and reduce the page's ranking.

To avoid this, perform a more specific job, which is a web mapping. You can use a spreadsheet in Excel and make a column with the old URL, another with the new one.

Address Google knows and will be changed or deleted	New address for the content
www.myrestaurant.com/pekin-duck	www.myrestaurant.com/menu-dinner/pekin-duck

Once you list all URL changes, you should establish '301' redirections from the left column URLs to the ones on the right. A '301' redirection is a code that means the redirection is permanent. It tells Google, from the first time its robots are heading towards an old URL, that it has been changed forever and they should now go to a new URL to reach the same content.

From there, search engine algorithms will correct these URLs on their indexes. They will understand the content and results previously associated to the old address migrated to the new URL.

There are several WordPress *plugins* that allow you to make the migration easier. One of them is 301 Redirect Plugin, which allows you to introduce two columns, like the previous table.

20. TOOLS TO AUDIT THE SEO OF A WEBSITE

SCREAMING FROG

Probably the most used tool by SEO professionals and being one of the most powerful free software for SEO technical analysis for a website: Screaming Frog.

With it, you will have a complete audit of any web URL. It can be from your own business, from a specific page on your site, or from competitors to find out their strengths which may cause Google to choose them in its results above you.

Just download it from: https://www.screamingfrog.co.uk/seo-spider/ (for both Windows and Mac), and enter a URL in the top search bar. It won't take you too long for you to get used to navigating the dashboard and its different zones:

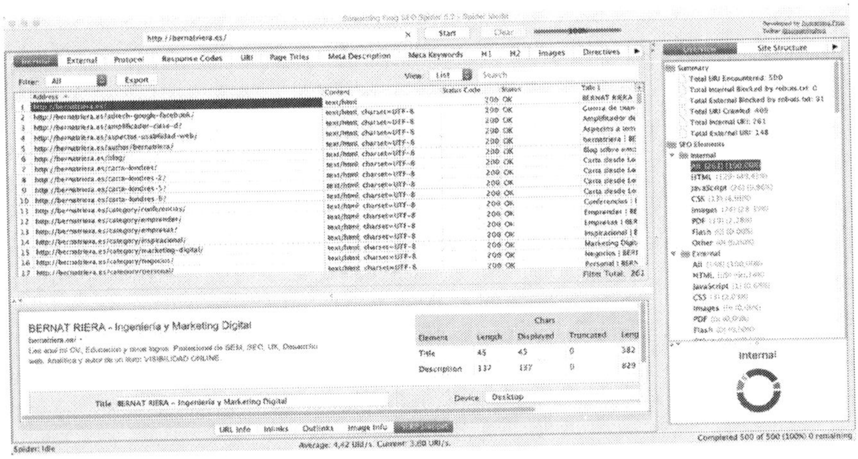

Central area: where you can browse different tabs to see the list of URLs with different information according to the columns displayed on the table. For example, if you want to see the titles, click on 'page titles' tab, or if you want to see the headers, click 'h1' or 'h2' tabs.

Right-hand side: a panel to find a summary and filtered by categories, to quickly detect what may be wrong and that you should start solving. I, for example, always go straight to see if:

- Titles and descriptions. Check if you have pages with duplicated titles or descriptions, and if they exceed the maximum number of characters or pixels recommended by Google (more than 65 characters or 487 pixels), as it could be shown cut when your website is displayed in its search results; or if, on the contrary, they are too short (less than 30 characters or 300 pixels), where in this case Google could automatically generate the descriptions from your content. You can see a preview of how it will appear on Google by clicking on the tab in the lower menu 'SERP snippet', allowing you to run tests of titles and descriptions to see which one works better in the results and try to get more clicks.
- Response codes. It is important to recognise which response your website gives each time someone accesses a page, file, image or document. These codes can be:
    - 200 – Page loads correctly.
    - 404 - Page not found. So, you should tell Google that this page has been moved to another address through a '301' or '302' redirection. Or if the content has been deleted instead of moved, then tell Google not to index this address any further. You can do this through the robots.txt file (Step 3).
    - 302 – Temporary redirection. This code means this content is now temporarily in another URL, but also Google shouldn't forget the previous URL since at a certain moment the content will be there again.
    - 301 – 301 Redirects are permanent and indicate that the content or address indexed by Google is now located elsewhere. Google will update its records, so they do not

re-crawl this URL, and instead it will be going to the new one directly.

- 500 – Server error. The page could not be accessed or the website is down. Fixing pages with this problem should be a priority.

- H1 and H2 Headings: it also analyses them and warns you if they are not optimised. The ideal structure is to have a single H1 and the minimum number of H2's (one or two if possible), so with this analysis, you will see if you have several H1's, or even worse, if you do not have any. It would be like having news without a title or subtitle.
- Images: Evaluate the number of images you have and how big they are checking their KB's or MB's, which will directly impact the loading time of your page. The information like ALT tag or title/description you give to Google about these images will also be taken into account for organic ranking since robots (like from Google itself), or people that cannot properly see, the images will only have this text to obtain information about what you are showing.
- Response Times: It groups the number of pages that are loaded in a certain number of seconds. You want the bar graph to be descended, meaning that most of your pages are loaded in less than 1 second.
- Structure: it tells how deep your structure is. It guides you about the current depth levels of your website, how many pages are under pages and pages (or folders and folders). For example, the 'drinks' page is at a 4th level depth, and may not be necessary: http://barmayor.com/dinner/menu/drinks/

Bottom area:

It gives you all the details about the selected URL, from the internal links that you get from other internal or external pages, plus to how it is indexed and displayed on Google in its SERP Snippet tab.

Reports from ScreamingFrog

Screaming Frog allows you to export in CSV tables all the information so you can easily process, filter, and evaluate it in Excel. For example, I created a report for my SEO clients in which I download all of the information from Screaming Frog, paste it into Excel and it then updates my report and quickly audit the site to identify quick wins that can have a very positive impact on its SEO ranking, such as missing headings, duplications, or not optimum number of characters on the titles.

You could also copy and paste this information into Google Docs and import it into the reports mentioned above, such as Google Data Studio or SuperMetrics.

EXTENSIONS FOR GOOGLE CHROME

With these additional Google Chrome extensions, you can get extra information about the site you are optimizing. To install these extensions, you only need to go to the Chrome extension store, search for it and install it in your browser.

Brokenlinks chrome

With a single click, you can analyse any webpage you are in and see if there are links to any other pages, both internal and external, those do not load properly or lead to a 404 error.

It will show you all the links of that web either in red (broken) or green (which work correctly).

Webmaster Tool Bar

It is a complete tool that will allow you to easily identify the structure of headings from a page (H1, H2 ...), in a very clear visual way. Click on its 'Information' tab followed by '*View Document Outline*'.

In addition to this, you will observe multiple functions, such as changing the screen resolution, disabling page elements like CSS, images or cookies to detect if any of them is causing problems.

Firebug

A well-known tool among webmasters that allows you to inspect and identify elements from a web and to know where it is in the website's code, so you can easily find it and modify it.

For example, when you open it and click 'Inspect', you can move the cursor over the web to select the item you would like to inspect, for example, the navigation menu. Once it's clicked, it will show you its HTML code on the left and its CSS code on the right side, where you can even change it to other values to simulate it on your browser before making the change. If you are happy with it, then you can find that line of code from a specific file that you can get through your FTE folders and change it so that it has a real effect.

ColorZilla

With an intuitive drop count, you can move your cursor through any web and identify the Hexadecimal colour of any pixel that you would like to use in the future in your web or graphic designs.

Gosthery

This extension shows you all the codes of third parties that any website has in it. These could be remarketing codes, Google conversions codes, among many others. It is useful to check if your codes are firing correctly, or if you visit another page, you will know about their cookies tracking you.

21. THE NEAR FUTURE OF SEO

Thanks to all the new technology we embrace every day into our processes, ranking your company on the digital world will change a lot in the coming years, or months.

NATIVE APP SEARCHES WILL INCREASE

Searches will be done more often on native apps directly, which will offer complete experiences and solutions to their users. For example, Facebook, WhatsApp, Google Maps, Airbnb, or Amazon. This will lead to responses slightly influenced by the ecosystem or social network they are in. Google will no longer monopolise the 'best results source'. It will be a lot more diversified.

To keep being well ranked, your effort should go above and beyond. You will need to ensure your website has a mobile version (this should be obvious by now), but also, to keep in mind all these apps and systems when designing it. For example, include a button on your mobile version to 'share on WhatsApp', which shares the link with your user's cell phone contacts. Integrating apps with your website will definitely make it easier to locate you if one of them searches for a restaurant on a specific app. Yours could be the first choice if you understood that ecosystem and the integration with contacts, heart rates, locations and others.

PAID TRAFFIC WILL DOMINATE GOOGLE'S RESULTS

In 2017 most search results are still organic, aside from the first 4 positions. Which means almost everything we see before scrolling down are advertisements. Google search engine will move this way in the coming years, for sure.

No matter how much effort you put in optimizing your website because even if you manage to rank number 1 among SEO search results, you probably won't be the first link users see. But don't worry, your efforts and SEO techniques won't be in vain:

- Many users use *ad blockers*, this makes ads disappear and organic results become the first options.
- SEO techniques and usability shouldn't just be used to improve your rank on Google. They also allow you to offer a better experience for visitors.
- If you start an advertising campaign and paying to send traffic to a specific landing page, it will be, probably, poorer in optimization and content than your main website. So, if you apply the principles explained on this stage, Google will increase your *Quality Score* and charge you less per click.

OPTIMISE YOUR WEBSITE TO BE READ EASILY

Wearables, augmented reality and holograms are here to stay and expand. Your desktop computer and laptop will get new competitors every day, which will reduce their use.

Web experience on smaller screens, or even interfaces without screens, will make interaction with these devices increasingly voice-based. So, if you want to be a few steps ahead, make sure your website can be read and understood easily by a robot.

To get that, make sure you integrate recognizable phone numbers, maps, with integrated addresses, images, and videos. All these elements with their particular descriptions and attributes.

Soon, holograms will be settled and screens will be projected on any surface at any time. Maybe produced by these *wearables*. Design and usability will be protagonists, and we will have to adapt again.

To conclude, stay up to date on new technologies. Analyse their results and services when you use them or ask them a query. Keep optimizing your site, adapting it to new voice-based assistants like Amazon's Alexa and Google Home, which connect your home automation, do online searches and read all the information to the user.

Source: Microsoft

STEP 4

ONLINE ADVERTISING

22. GET RESULTS TODAY WITH ONLINE ADVERTISING

Here is one of the clearest messages I will give you in this book, and one which you should trust if you want to kick start your online (or even physical) business as soon as possible in order to start making money: Invest in online advertising campaigns. As we progress I will explain in which channels to invest, as well as when and how much, for you to gain the confidence that you need when investing and choosing the appropriate platform for your business.

Many entrepreneurs want to invest in a lot of things rather than online advertising, and it has always seemed to me that they leave the most important investment to last.

First, they decide to work on paperwork, hiring people (who do not initially have much to do), renting and decorating an office instead of growing their client portfolio and their revenue streams to balance their initial negative cash flow during the first months.

If you have $100, $500, $1,000 or more and you are thinking about what would be best to spend it on, then the answer is usually to make sure that when customers have a need that you can cover, they are able to find you. And that means buying the available advertising space on Google. It may be hard to start, but as soon as you see results, you will not stop investing and having active campaigns.

WHICH ONLINE CHANNEL SHOULD YOU PROMOTE YOUR BUSINESS ON?

Below, I will show you your clients' natural buying cycle, which applies regardless of your purpose.

Users who don't want to buy right now are in a passive state of the cycle, but it is important that you educate them about your brand and proposition even before they need you.

When the need arises for whatever reason, then the proactive search cycle part begins, and competition between companies becomes more aggressive to capture that potential customer who is ready to buy.

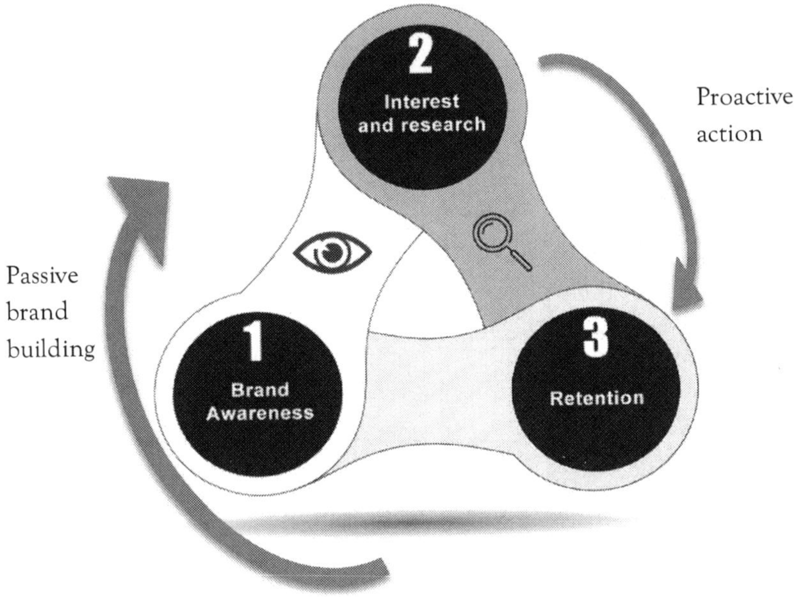

Finally, once the purchase has been made and the customer's immediate need has ceased, it is time to retain them, to lead them to buy more or upgrade their product after a while. It is also necessary to make them become your best promotional voice for the people they influence.

These are the buying stages described in more detail:

Stage 1: Brand recognition and slow persuasion

The first thing your customers will have to do is find out that your product or service exists, and then you must educate them on why they should be interested specifically in you, and why they should buy from you.

The less well known your product or brand is compared to your competitors, the stronger your investment should be. It may be hard to see the direct return of this investment, but in the long run it is a necessary one.

There are several valuable online channels for getting this brand recognition and generating interest when your potential customers are not yet actively interested in buying what you sell. These are Facebook, Twitter, Instagram, Display, Gmail and YouTube, and I will explain how to create winning campaigns in all of them.

Stage 2: Interest and search

There will be a trigger, or a specific moment in which users actively want what you sell. This may be due to a need you have created (a new app), or because some condition has changed and now they need to purchase something they did not need before (their TV broke and they need to buy a new one, or their back hurts and they need a physical therapist).

When this moment happens, the first natural place your users will go to is a search engine, mainly Google, to see who offers that service in their area. This is when you should ensure you appear for any combination of words that they enter in the search bar.

75% of purchases of any kind (both online and offline), and for both: product or service, start in some way in the search engines.

Another factor to bear in mind when planning your campaign is the competition that you have – not only physical, but also online. Who is advertising when you search for your product on Google? If you still do not know, then stop, take out your mobile phone, and google it. Yes, exactly: now and on the phone. This is how your potential client will search for it. It doesn't matter if you're selling T-shirts through an Ecommerce site or if you sell electric generators to power an entire town. The first step is to look for some initial information from anywhere – and a synonym of 'anywhere' is from their mobile phones.

Do you see that result with a green icon that says 'Ad' appearing in the first position? Is it you? It should be!

Stage 3: Retention

Once a customer clicks on your ad, you must provide the easiest and most direct path to purchase or conversion – but I'll explain how to perfect this in the section about 'Usability'.

At this moment two things can happen: either they become your client or they do not. In each case, it is recommended that you retarget them with new ads. If they are already clients, you can invite them to loyalty programs or upsell more products to them. If they didn't buy in the first place, try to catch their interest again through personalised messages in order to convince them next time.

ESTABLISHING CAMPAIGN OBJECTIVES AND HOW WE MEASURE SUCCESS

Identify how you will measure the success of your website. Is it by number of sales of a certain product to demonstrate its market penetration, or do you care less about the volume and more whether they are buying the most expensive products?

In other cases, you may be more interested in the number of times your ad is viewed or clicked to get an idea of how customers react to your brand when they see your image or advertisement, so success might be determined by the number of impressions or clicks to your website.

Clearly defining your objective also means you can start with that goal in mind and be clear on what you want to achieve. You will see that once you decide the end of the road, it will be much easier to visualise the route to it. Perhaps you need to focus your strategy only on certain channels or products, since anything that takes a customer away from the goal will be a waste of time or money.

23. ADS IN GOOGLE SEARCH

GOOGLE ADWORDS: PAID SEARCH

There are business owners who are still confused by the assumption that if their business is for other companies (B2B) and not for end consumers (B2C), then they should not be advertising on Google. But it is a very common mistake not to realise that decision makers in small or large companies are people, and their starting point is still the same as yours or mine – to google it! In fact, if older decision makers do not google, they are still influenced by younger team members or technicians who do.

Google should be the basis of all online advertising campaigns. As we have established earlier in the SEO phase, presence and visibility in Google is fundamental.

Even if you are organically in the top position, you should invest in Google AdWords to make sure a competitor does not appear above you in the first paid positions of Google, which are the slots appearing above the organic results, the ones getting the click and the sale.

Look at the next screenshot. Autotrader.co.uk is the first organic result but it's appearing in fourth place because of the three ads above it. Actually, the second paid result is also theirs. This is a clear example of having a good organic position and knowing that they need to buy ads to compete in that top space too.

I've heard a lot of people say that nobody clicks on Google ads, and then I've seen them using the Internet and it turns out they do click on ads, but they don't even realise it. It is becoming increasingly difficult to distinguish between an ad and a free result on Google.

From my long experience in the online marketing world, I can assure you that yes, people click a lot on ads, and the companies I've worked for spend millions of dollars a year on this. I've also spent my own money to support my websites and once you start, you do not stop investing, since capturing the opportunity of potential customers looking on Google is very important and profitable.

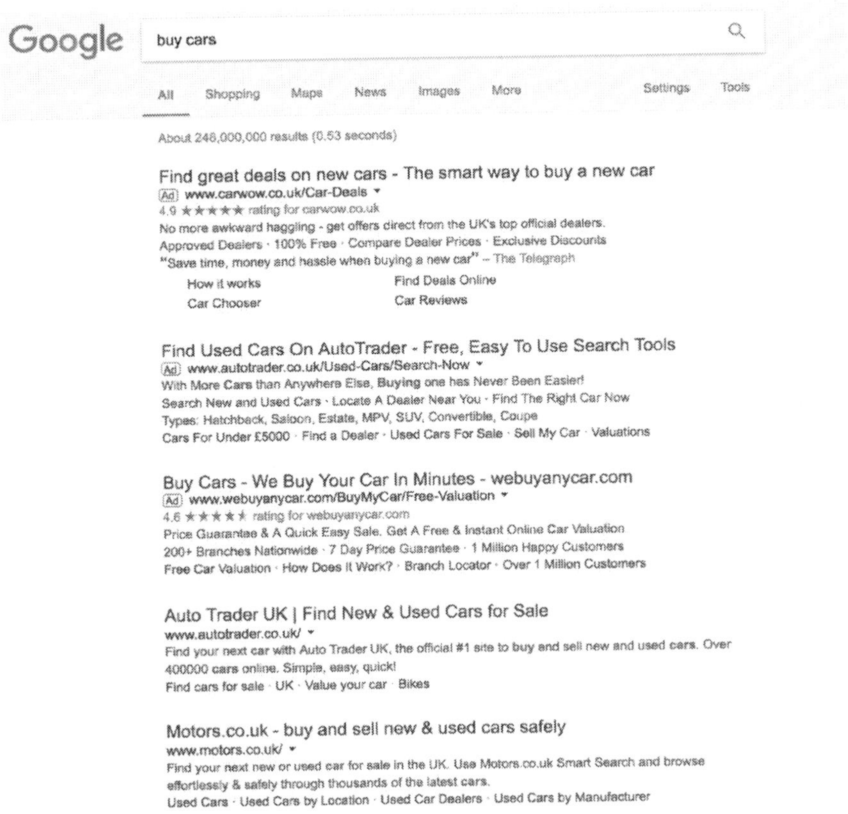

Advertise in search engines if your customers can search on the Internet for your services or products. If you sell a product that already exists (e.g. shoes), customers will look for somewhere to buy it, either online (website with the best deals on shoes) or by searching for a store in their location to make the purchase in person (shoe store near Hammersmith). If it is a service, the search will probably be accompanied by the name of a neighbourhood, city or country.

When we talk about customers searching, these are 'potentials' from the beginning, because we know they are already looking for that product or service, they already have a need and they are interested in paying to fulfil it. Just make sure to be there at the right time.

It is important to know that you will be paying nothing every time someone searches for you and your ad appears. You will only pay when someone clicks on it. This means you may have 1,000 impressions (times your ad is shown) per day, but if you only have one click from a user, the only thing you'll pay Google for is that single click. The cost can range from €0.01 to €20, depending on the competition for that keyword and how relevant your ad and website are for that search, although you can limit this with the 'maximum bid' (max. CPC) that you are able to pay. If this is €0.5, you will not pay more than that per click, although if there are other companies with a higher maximum bid, then they will appear above you. Google, like the rest of online platforms, is an auction-based system and competitiveness maximises its benefit, of course.

Remember, Google rewards those who offer the best experience and are the best result for a specific search. Same principle applies to paid ads: the more relevant the ads are, the less you pay per click.

Developing and creating advertising campaigns on Google is very simple. Optimizing them and getting the best performance is not as easy, but don't worry, it isn't for your competitors either, and you will soon be able to take advantage of that. All details and steps will be explained in this chapter.

The diagram below shows the flow of a search action, an ad displaying a click with cost and sending the user to your chosen web page (your landing page).

CREATE SUCCESSFUL CAMPAIGNS ON GOOGLE ADWORDS

When do you want to appear on Google?

In order to advertise on Google, you must think about what words or key phrases you want to show in your ads and start writing a list on an Excel sheet. For example, if I want to promote a new book like this one, my list would look something like this:

```
Business books, SEO book, AdWords book, buy book marketing, usability guide, make money online, etc.
```

What budget do you have to invest initially (without knowing if you will have a return on the investment)?

If we are guaranteed that we will recover €100 for every euro invested, who would not want to invest without limits? But the return on investment is not guaranteed at this point, so in your first campaign, consider incremental budgets that you can take as losses until you are able to identify exactly how many of your new clients came through your adverts, and you are completely sure it makes sense to re-invest.

In which continent, country or city are the users you wish to show your ads to?

You must be very careful not to show your ads to irrelevant people. Depending on your business, these may be people in your neighbourhood, city, region or country, so you must select the geographical location of your ads carefully. So if you own a pharmacy, you will be keen to target your campaign to those near your area rather than more broadly to the whole city—unless, for example, you offer a significantly different service from the other pharmacies in town.

What do you want to happen once customers enter your keywords into a search engine?

Once you have gained the opportunity to appear, it will be up to you to decide the message you display, as you have to capture the customer's attention and take the only click they make on the screen. You must also decide where to send them after that and the experience they will have on your website once they land.

If you have these basic points in your mind, you already have 70% of the campaign worked out. Now you only need the technical implementation that we will now be working through step by step.

Create an Account in Google AdWords

Go to adwords.google.com and sign in with your usual Gmail account. If you already have one, log in with that, or if not then go ahead and create a new one.

There is also a method to create a Google AdWords account with the address of your company, but you have to take a previous step which is to associate your professional email with a Google account. You can do this through the following link:
https://accounts.Google.com/SignUpWithoutGmail

When you finally have signed in and taken your first steps through the account, Google will guide you on how to create your first campaign, ad, group of keywords, etc. I would recommend that you skip the tutorial (at the beginning you will find a 'skip' button) and head straight to the main interface for which I will give you all the information you need. Otherwise, some people end up creating a campaign without even knowing what they are doing, set up the payment and start spending money before they realise. If you already see yourself there, do not worry; create an account, put a budget of €1 and set the payment, but immediately after it has been created, pause it until you fully understand how everything works.

STRUCTURE OF CAMPAIGNS AND AD GROUPS

It is important to know the levels in an AdWords account, which will allow you to make better or worse optimizations as well as performance and budget management, depending on the structures.

It all starts by grouping the different keywords you have in the account, so each specific group of keywords will also have an ad related to them. For instance, if you sell cars, you may have a group of keywords related to the brand BMW and all ads in that ad group will also contain BMW on the headline or description, so it's all relevant across keywords and ads.

In addition, thinking that one ad will be perfect at capturing the attention of all users is very naive, so it is important to have several ads rotating to discover which performs best. One might talk about a car's efficiency and low consumption, and another about its speed, for example.

All of these words and relevant ad variations are grouped into an 'Ad Group'.

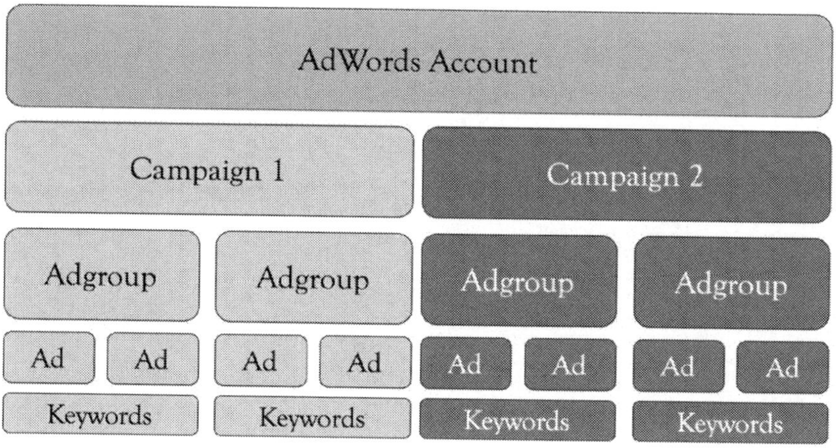

Now that you've created messages and words for the car brands you sell in your ad groups, they need to be grouped into your top level 'Campaigns', which have special and important configuration properties that we'll cover below, such as daily budget and geographical situation, among others. So a good idea, in the example of cars, would be to create a separate campaign for the two centres you have, one in London and another in Manchester. Or another strategy could be to create campaigns for high-end, low-end, second-hand and rental cars. The configurations are infinite.

When designing the structure of your campaigns in your Google AdWords account, it will help you keeping these three points in mind:

1. Clear at a glance: You have to be able to identify in a few seconds the strategy followed, the division that has been made and its granularity.
2. It is scalable: The structure has to be arranged in such a way that it can grow according to the products, demand, services, channels, localities or budget, among other factors.
3. Use a naming system in which it is easy to generate data for your analysis, so that when you download the statistics by

campaign, it is quick and easy to filter the information you want with Excel.

Campaign and Ad Group Settings

One of the differentiating points between campaign and ad group is that the former control the daily budget. With campaigns you can also select the country and language in which you want to show your ads.

Campaigns should be aligned with your business goals, and placing an individual daily budget on each campaign will allow you to invest more or less in the brand, in certain products, in the most profitable services or in those that need a push.

The settings you will only be able to make at campaign level are:

- **Daily budget:** This is one of the most important ones. Here you must divide what you want to spend per month and per day by the total number of campaigns. You should know that Google can exceed that daily limit by 20%, assuming that on another day you will spend less, in order to ensure you do not miss the opportunity to capture those searches. For example, spend a little more on the weekdays, as you can expect to spend less on Saturday and Sunday.
- **Type:** You must choose 'Search only' if you only want to advertise on Google. If, on the other hand, you want to expand into the Display Network, you can also select 'Display Network'. But make sure you read my chapter on Display (GDN) first, as it will be very easy for you to spend money on this channel if you do not pay close attention to what you are doing.
- **Delivery method:** This can be set to Standard (that is, distributing the daily budget throughout the day) or Accelerated (to appear in Google as much as possible until you spend your whole budget). In the second case, depending on your keywords and budget, you could spend your daily budget in a few hours.

- **Start and end date:** Very useful to create certain promotions during a specific period of time.

Ad groups, on the other hand, allow you to set the same bid (maximum cost per click) for all keywords in them. However, I do not recommend doing that, since the keywords may have different relevance and competitiveness in Google, so it is preferable to bet on them at word level.

ADS AND EXTENSIONS

The ads you write will be the customer-facing impression of all the work you have done behind the scenes. They are what your customers will see, what will compete in Google with other advertisers – and only one of them will be clicked.

They should be relevant, easy to read, and draw the users' attention so they choose to click on your ad. Tell them what you offer (Massages in Paris), what they will find after the click (Book online now, ask for prices and times, etc.), and show your advantages compared to the competition (20% discount first appointment).

From my experience, I would say that considering how fast the Internet is today, people tend to click on the first result that appears, almost instinctively, and if they know that it is not what they are looking for, it takes them just a second to go back and click on the next result. So be strong in the message of your ad for those users who still read, but also remember that for those who do not, being in the first position can make a difference in getting that click.

I would even say that many click and open different tabs in their browser for as many as the first five or six results, and then they will take a look at each to see if that page offers what they wanted, so creating a good landing page will be very important to retain their attention.

The ad will play an important role in the final cost per click you pay, as defined by the 'Ad rank', a parameter that evaluates the relevance of the ad for the keywords contained in its message as related to the search that the user made, and with it, the final landing page – both the URL and its content.

Ad rank is a formula, but I will not tell you how it is calculated because you'll never remember it. Just remember the following:

- The ad contains keywords preferably in the title, but also in the description.
- The display URL looks as similar as possible to the destination URL, and if they also contain a keyword, that's even better.
- Try to get the highest number of clicks with a well-described action (like 'Start Today for Free') and try to raise your maximum bet to show your ad above the competition. Both will positively affect your CTR (click through rate). The higher, the better.
- Everything is relevant for Google, from the initial keyword, to the ad, to the final content of the website.

The CTR is a percentage that defines how often an ad has been clicked divided by the total number of times it has been shown. So if your ad shows 100 times, and only gets five clicks, the CTR is of 5%.

To set up a good ad, it is recommended that you use all the allowed characters. These are:

- Title 1: 30 characters
- Title 2: 30 characters
- Description line: 80 characters
- 2 x visible URL addresses: 35 characters

Search example: 'bluetooth speakers from Amazon'

AD EXTENSIONS TO INCREASE REAL STATE

Using ad extensions will be very important to give a faster reaction experience to users looking for something specific, such as a phone or specific pages within a website (such as the contact section or prices). But in addition, you will be increasing your physical space in the results page, which in itself is very good for increasing your CTR.

Next, I will explain the best extensions available, but it's important that you always keep your eyes open for Google's updates. You can find them in the 'Ad extensions' section.

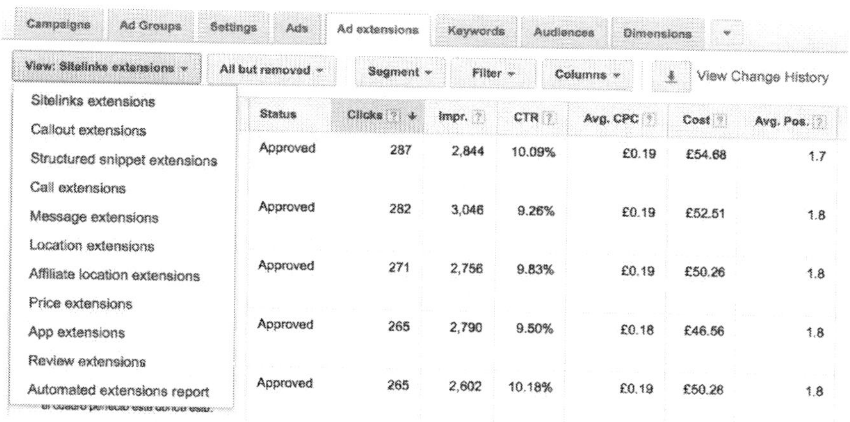

Sitelinks

Sitelinks will allow you to double or triple your space in the search results, adding direct links below the main ad to other pages within the destination website.

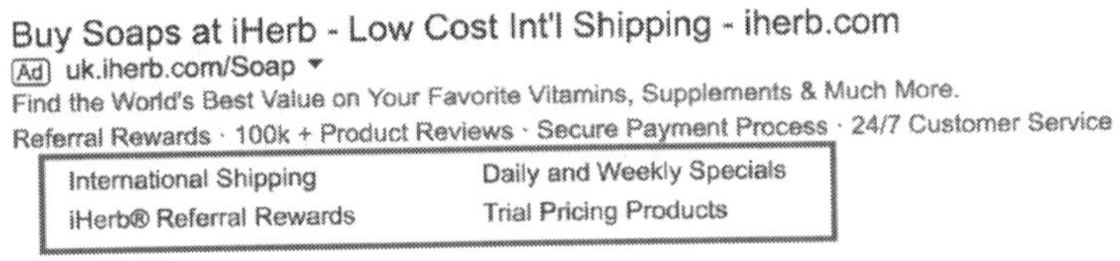

The links will show mainly when your ad appears in the first position but not 100% of the time. In addition, depending on the search and other conditions, Google may display only the title of the link (such as the previous iherb advert shown) and not alongside their descriptions.

The character limit is different from normal ads. The title will have only 25 letters and two descriptive lines of 35 characters each. Another difference from normal ads is that they do not have a visible web address.

The final destination of each of these links must be necessarily different, and you can use them for specific products or offers, a contact page, your blog, etc.

Like ads, these links can be pre-configured to serve on mobile devices rather than on computers, and it's important to know how to prevent your links from being shortened when they are displayed on smaller screens. So, for mobile, you can limit yourself to using 15 characters per title and description line.

Callouts and Structured Snippet Text

These extensions allow you to gain two lines of space in your displayed ad. You can add features of your product or service offered without them being linkable, as text only.

The callout text will be displayed as words separated by dots or hyphens, and the structured snippets will be under a word describing the list, like 'types' on the example.

Telephone

Keep in mind that this feature is different from when you create a page on Google+, in that your company's phone number appears in the organic results on the right and people can call you with a click.

Here we are in the payment section, and this extension will add a 'Call' button below your ad. This is very important if your goal, for example, is for people to search for 'cab Hammersmith' and you can show your number with a telephone icon and button. It is a perfect extension for those who have searched from their mobile to see that option – it is ideal for them to click it and make a reservation without having to navigate through more results or websites.

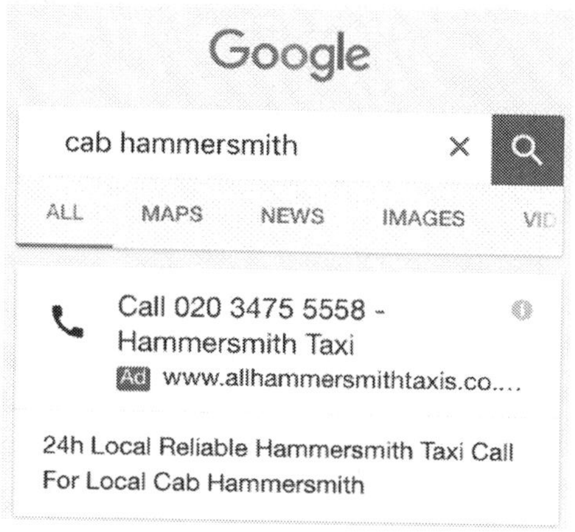

You can find this extension in 'Ad extensions' / 'Telephone'.

It is important to program the extension of the phone so that it is only available at a time when you can answer calls, and that it is only shown on mobile devices. When creating the extension, you will be asked for a schedule, and you can even configure different phones at different times. You may be able to receive calls on your mobile when you are not in the office.

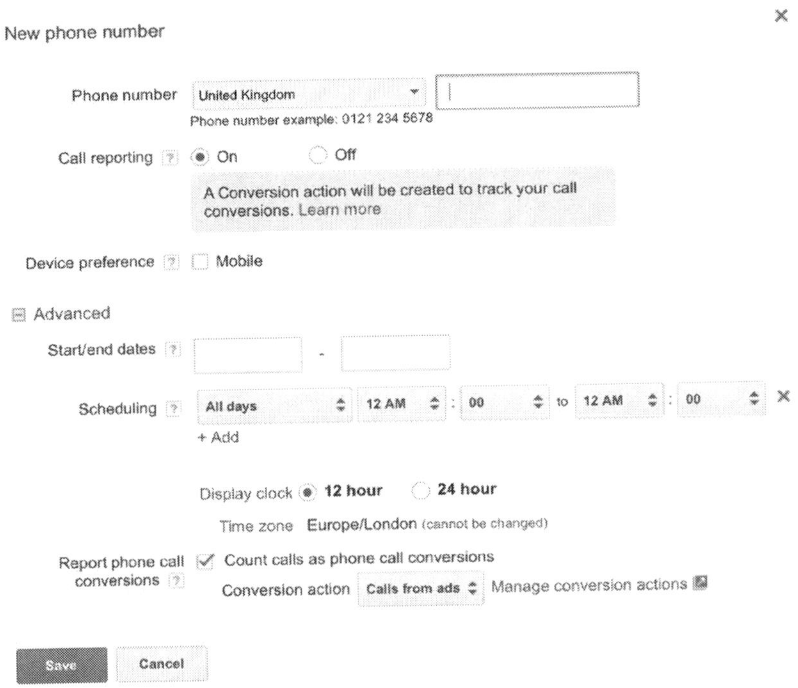

Geographic Location

This extension can be very quick and useful if you have already created a directory entry in Google MyBusiness with all your stores, restaurants, or other locations where you offer your service. You will only need to link the two accounts and enter your email and password into '+ Extension'.

If, on the other hand, you do not have this set up, and you just want to create one or two locations, you can also add them on AdWords manually.

Once activated, when users search for your service in a city where you have your location extensions, the Google ad will appear, and from a mobile they will get directions on how to get to you with a single click.

The disadvantage of this extension is that users can click on the map link (and you pay for the click), but this directs them to the map and not to your website, so you may be losing the lead you expected with that user by converting them into a new customer. However, it is important to know this in terms of analysing the performance of your ads.

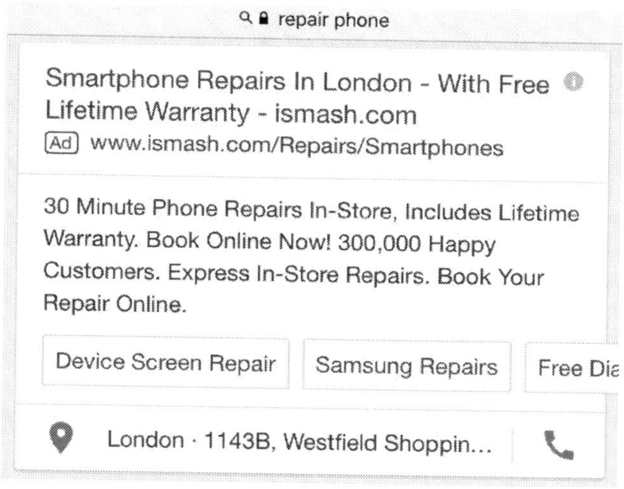

KEYWORDS AND MATCH TYPES

Keywords are the triggers for showing your ads, which will relate to the search made by the user and the words they have entered in Google which are theoretically related to your website or business.

You can have many different keywords, which should be grouped into different ad groups where all grouped phrases have a similar meaning.

It is not necessary to consider all the possible combinations a user can make in the search box (basically because they could be infinite); it is enough to understand the different concordances of the keywords to cover a greater number of possibilities, such as 'Exact' or 'Broad'. However, remember that the more relevant your keywords are to the search that has been made, as well as the ad and the landing page, the more you will be rewarded by Google and the less you will pay per click.

In the second chapter of Phase 1, we already saw how to use the Google AdWords 'Keyword Planner' tool, and here it can also be very useful for developing a long initial list of keywords that you can then filter or expand according to how relevant they are to your business.

Exact Match

'Exact match' means the words you have to focus your strategy on the most. Betting with exact words means that your ads will only appear when a user search exactly matches the keyword, including the same words and being in the same order.

There is an additional box where you can indicate whether you allow Google to consider spelling or plural errors as exact or strictly different.

The keywords in exact match will be the words with the highest QS (Quality Score), since they should be much more relevant, both to the text used in the ad and to the landing page, and will not take into consideration another possible combination of words that might be less relevant.

To indicate this match type, Google uses the symbols [ ].

Keywords	Your ad will show for	Your ad will not show for
[cooking courses]	cooking courses	Courses cooking Courses on cooking Courses to cook better Cook courses Courses and videos cooking Buy cooking courses Online cooking courses Download cooking courses Free videos and cooking Cooking courses in London

Broad Match Modifier

This is like the enhanced version of broad match type, which may be too generic, as you give Google a lot of freedom to show your ad for a lot of words or combinations outside of your control. Google will look for just a few of the words, and even if they're just similar, the ad will trigger, and maybe you will spend a lot on clicks in searches that were not very relevant.

The 'modifier' version consists of putting a plus symbol '+' in front of the words that *must* appear in the search bar for Google to show your ad, or it will not otherwise be shown. The + symbol does not have to be in all words, as some may not be as necessary as others.

As you can see, we are getting closer to results increasingly related to our activity, just by telling Google which words should be there or not.

Keywords	Your ad will show for	Your ad will not show for
+salsa +dance lessons	**Salsa dance lessons** **Dance salsa** classes YouTube **Dance salsa** **salsa dance**	Latin dance lessons Salsa lessons
+salsa +dance +lessons	**Salsa dance lessons** in London **Lessons** to **dance salsa** with couples	Salsa dance Salsa dance courses

NEGATIVE KEYWORDS

Negative keywords are as necessary as positive keywords, as long as you have keywords that are not only an exact match. That's because, both the phrase and broad match types, will attract different search combinations that you did not imagine in your initial strategy.

These tell Google that if that your negative keywords are in the user search bar then they must not show your ad.

For example, imagine that many people search for free online cooking courses, but the ones you offer on your page are not free, but must be paid per download.

Then all users who look for free courses and click on your ad will have a bad experience, because when you see the price or the 'buy' button, they will probably go back to Google for the next result. So, adding '-free' as a negative keyword, you make sure that you do not appear any more in searches with that word.

This example is an obvious one that you had no doubt already thought about when designing your strategy, but as you continue to optimise, you will discover all the possible combinations of words that your ads show. It is important to review them frequently and add important negative keywords whenever you find an irrelevant, expensive or low CTR one.

For example, I would not be surprised if you find 'torrent' next to your keyword 'download Photoshop courses' (for those who do not know, torrent is a system used for free downloads, usually including illegal content), so you may also add the negative '-torrent'.

Negative words can be added at both the ad group and campaign level, affecting all positive words within those levels.

If we return to the example described in the words phrase, we have now added the negative '-free':

Keywords	Your ad will show for	Your ad will not show for
'cooking courses' -free	Buy cooking courses Online cooking courses Download cooking courses Cooking courses in London	Free courses cooking Courses free to cook better Cook courses Cooking videos and courses Free cooking courses and videos

Negatives can also have different matches (broad, phrase, or exact) and allow you to adjust your results to the user's intent and search.

Match types for negative keywords

Negative exact: Google will only avoid showing your ad for that particular ad group or campaign when the search is exactly matched with the negative.

Negative	Your ad will show for	Your add will not show for
-[new cars]	New red cards Semi-new cars Second hand cards New cars magazine	New cars

Negative broad: These negatives will block any combination of searches that contain them. If there is more than one word as negative (like the following example: '-new cars'), your ad won't show when both words are in the search, regardless of the order. If only one of the words is searched (*cars*), your ad would appear because *cars* it's considered a different term than *new cars*.

Negative	Your ad will show for	Your ad will not show for
-new cars	Used motorcycles Buy vehicles	New red cars Cars new Buy new cars Where to buy cheap new cars Almost new cars Cars new upholstery New GPS for cars

I recommend that you create a campaign by match type (making all broad keywords in a 'Broad' campaign or all exact in an 'Exact' campaign) to avoid an instance of your campaign daily budget being eaten by broad match (less relevant) rather than exact match (cheaper and usually with better results).

SEARCH TERMS

Often our broad match keywords will show our ads for searches that are not entirely relevant, and it is our task to optimise those campaigns to maintain their quality and relevance.

Google AdWords offers us the ability to see all the actual searches that have been done behind those keywords through the 'Keywords' / 'Search results' / 'See details' tab, where we are able to select only some or all of the keywords.

I recommend ordering all those searches by number of impressions because of the 20/80% rule, which refers to 80% of the results being determined by only 20% of the keywords. So, if you optimise the words or searches that generate more impressions, you'll easily improve the overall performance of the campaign, without having to waste time through the other words that only made one impression one day and may not be searched anymore.

Add Negatives

You must identify search terms that have triggered our keywords by their similarity, but which in fact are irrelevant to our product. Once you select those terms, you can add them as negative keywords at different levels (in ad group or campaign one) by clicking on 'add as negative keyword'.

By default, these will be added as exact negatives, but you can edit the [] symbols by adding a " " phrase or even have a broad match by leaving the words without symbols.

OPTIMISE YOUR CAMPAIGNS: REDUCE THE COST PER CLICK AND INCREASE RELEVANCE OR CTR

Relevance is what gets the most out of PPC (pay-per-click) campaigns, and Google makes to pay more to those advertisers who try to show their ads when neither the ad nor the page they offer to the user has much to do with what that person has searched for. You can still show the ad, but it will be more expensive.

There are several tricks to increase the CTR:

Increase your ad's position

It is statistically proven that when an ad is in the second position of the results, instead of the first position, it reduces your CTR by 14%, and when it goes down to 3rd, it drops exponentially to 33%. I don't longer need to continue with the ads that appear below the fold (portion of the website that you need to make an action to view it, like scrolling down) or even more extreme if we talk about the results on a mobile phone.

Explore your keywords and keep those very relevant, the ones you know that when a user searches for those exact terms, he must be a potential customer; and make sure that the keyword is shown in a high position. If not, increase your bid (max. CPC) gradually until you see that you are taking over that position.

If you have no idea how much your bid should be in order to reach that top position, you can add a new column to your AdWords dashboard called 'Est. top page bid' which suggests how much you should bid.

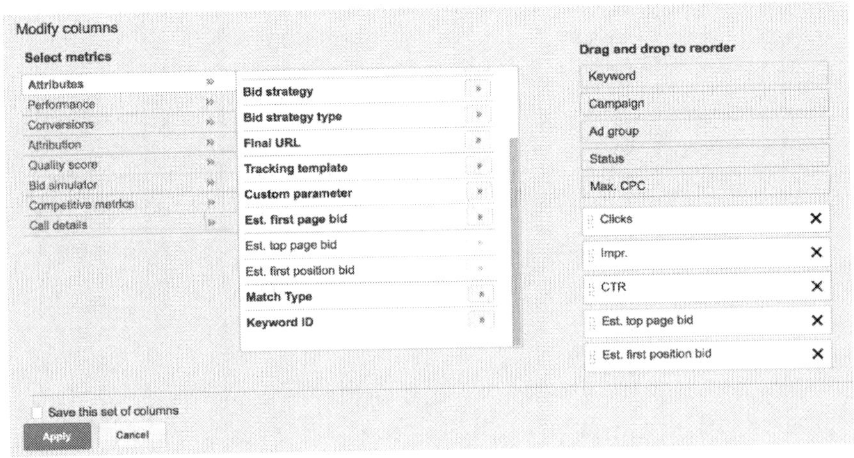

Sort your keywords by impressions again and find out which ones have a low average position each time they have been shown and try to improve them. The higher the number of impressions is, the more this will affect the average position of the keyword.

Change the ad

To increase CTR, it is important that every time you show your ad it has a high chance of being clicked. You only have one chance to catch that user, who may well be a great customer in the long term. Sounds great, does it not? Well, imagine that they click on your competitor. Improve your ad now and do not let them slip away.

You have to constantly test different ads and do not assume that you are already showing the best message. It may be the best message for you, but will almost certainly not be the best for every other person. I also do not know the magic recipe, but below you will see some best practices in writing ad copy so that a user, in 3 seconds, may decide to click on your ad and not your competitor's:

- Use all the available characters to occupy the largest real state on the results screen. 30 for title 1, 30 for title 2, and 80 for description, plus 2 display URL parts that will appear in green. This way you can tell your users where they will end up.
- Capitalise those important words so they can be read more easily.
- Use numbers when you can, as they attract attention and are read and understood more easily than words.
- Call to action: Assist the user in what they have to do next to encourage their click. E.g. 'Request appointment', 'Contact now', 'Buy cheap now'.
- Align the ads as much as you can to the keywords to make them appear marked in bold as they will match the text of your ad with the search query.
- Use the display URLs smartly adding some additional keywords also related to the search.

Optimising Cost Per Click (CPC)

To optimise CPC on a given word, you have to try to reduce the cost of that word, but as I said before, its cost will be affected by the average of all the costs of your search terms.

This time sort the list by clicks (rather than impressions) to determine which term brings a lot of traffic to your website at a very high cost per click, and evaluate if that search is relevant enough or not for your business for you to pay so much for it.

WORK OFFLINE: ADWORDS EDITOR

Google AdWords offers you a very powerful and free tool that allows you to manage your Google AdWords accounts using desktop software so you can work on them offline and make changes to many elements in a simpler and faster way.

Everything you do in this software will not be reflected in active campaigns until you post your changes online again. To download the platform, go to: https://www.google.com/intl/es/adwordseditor/ and follow the installation steps.

Once downloaded, go to 'Accounts' / 'Add' and you will be asked to enter your AdWords password. Below, you will see a complete listing of all the accounts you have access to. Select the ones you want to manage and download them.

The distribution of elements in the panel is very simple and you will get used to it very quickly. On the upper left side, you will see the list of campaigns and ad groups and in the lower left side, you can select what you want to see in the larger area on the right: keywords, negatives, ads, ad extensions, etc.

As you can see in the next screenshot, you can work offline with all types of campaigns you have online, including Search, Display, Remarketing and PLAs.

Selecting a keyword, ad or any other item will make it editable and you can change the match type, max. bid (max. CPC), status, destination URL, and other attributes.

To apply bulk changes, you first have to get the view of everything you want to change on the main screen, then select everything and apply the change. To get to see everything you want to, it is very important that you familiarise yourself with the search bar on top.

If you prefer the online platform for making optimisations because you can see there all the analysis data such as positions, impressions, clicks, etc., remember that you can also get this in Editor through the 'Statistics' button in the top menu, being able to select the range of time from which you want to view and download that data.

Do not forget to click on 'Publish' to make your changes effective.

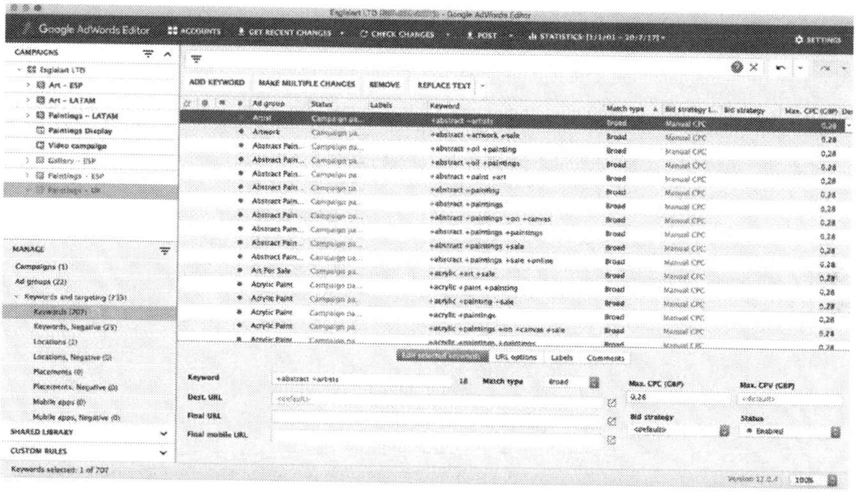

24. ADS IN GOOGLE DISPLAY NETWORK (GDN)

HOW TO SPREAD YOUR BRAND ACROSS OTHER WEBSITES

GDN advertising is the way to advertise through other websites relevant to your product by them showing your ad. It goes without saying that the more visual and attractive your ad is, the more clicks it will get.

The websites that can show your adverts (or those of other advertisers) are those that have signed up as participants to the Google AdSense program (where you can head to generate some euros, as I explained in Phase 1) and have placed ad spaces across their website.

The following example shows my visit to a car website, autotrader.com, where you can see the ad that Google has chosen to show me on the right.

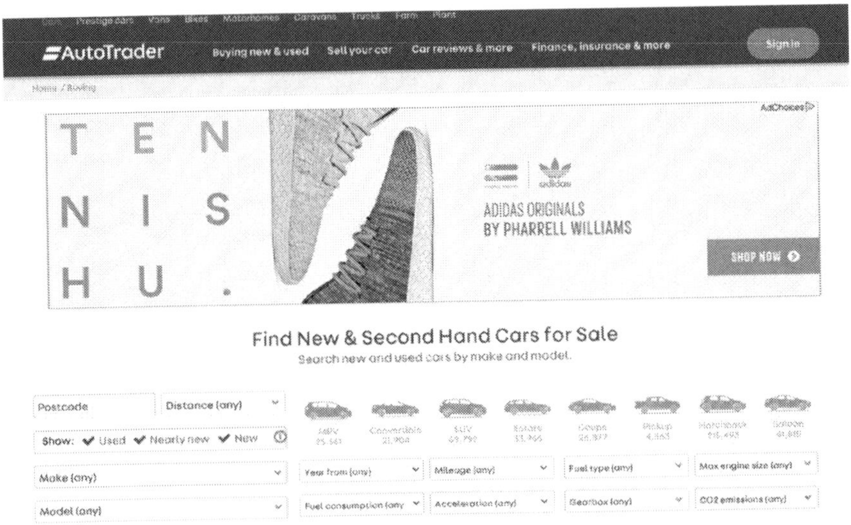

If you visit that website now, you will see a totally different ad, and it may be related to cars or something more specifically related to you, according to your earlier visits or the things Google knows about you from other browsing history.

In the above example, I had previously visited the Adidas website and they have remarketed me when I went to another web.

In AdWords you will create these ads to be displayed on other websites, and even if you do not have the design skills to create nice banners like the previous one, you can still place ads with text and images dynamically created on the AdWords platform.

You will also be able to decide on which sites you would like to display, as well as the bidding system you prefer, since here you have a choice other than CPC (cost per click), which is CPM (cost per thousand impressions). Your choice will depend on what you prefer to pay: either for visits to your website (CPC) or to show an advert as many times as possible, regardless of whether or not they click (CPM).

I always prefer to set the Display campaign to the normal CPC model, since if people see my ad but do not click, it does not contribute anything to me. But there are many brands looking to get as many people as possible to see their logo or their new product, so in the end it depends on your strategy.

As you see in the following drop-down menu, when creating a campaign, you can select one that has the option to advertise in Google search, as well as in Display.

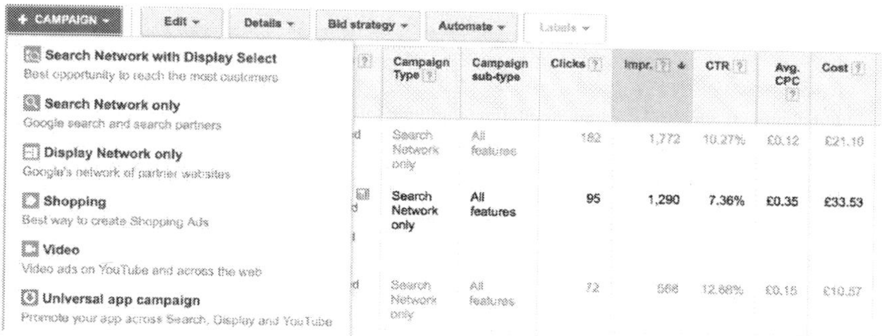

However, I recommend having separated search and display campaigns, and working on that channel exclusively, since you will soon see that they operate in a very different way in both, performance and cost.

The daily budget that you set for the Display campaigns will be completely spent, since the inventory of websites where Google can display your ad is very large. In addition, you may be showing your ad multiple times to the same person on different websites, so be sure to control this expense closely.

If it's your first campaign, you might see a guide like the one below, where you set your target. As I said before, these could get impressions (notoriety with CPM) or generate actions (sales and orders with CPC).

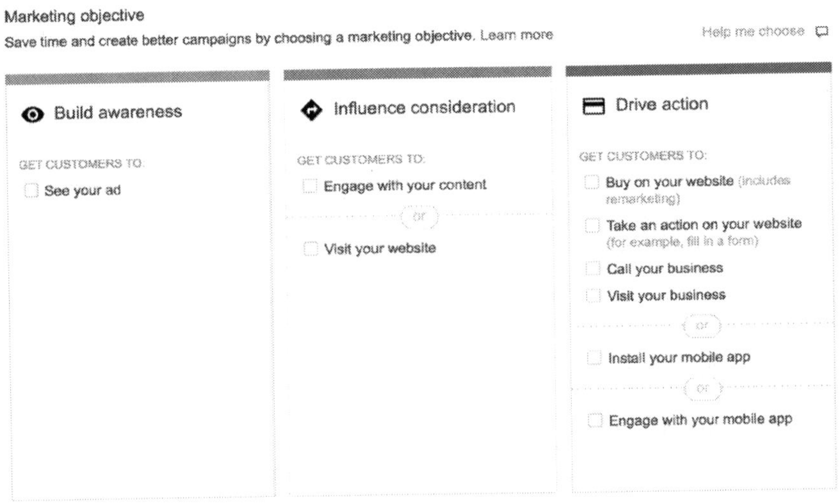

Once the campaign has been created, you'll need to select the targeting and the ads that will be displayed on the websites: you can create very interesting formats with the help of Google without many resources. Select '+ Ad' to see the options drop-down.

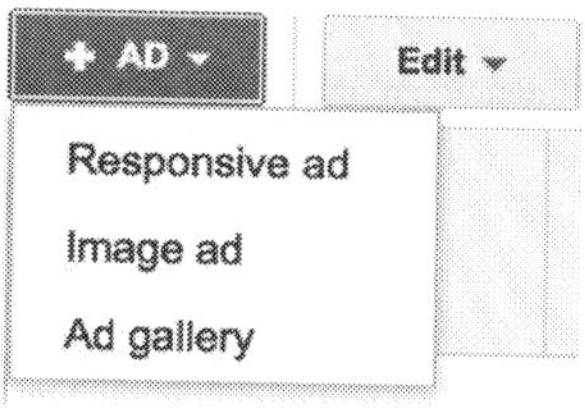

- **Responsive ad:** Allows you to create very interesting formats from a normal text ad with its titles and descriptions but adding an image and a logo that will allow Google to 'adapt' it to different websites and formats automatically, like the samples you see below after having created a new one very quickly.

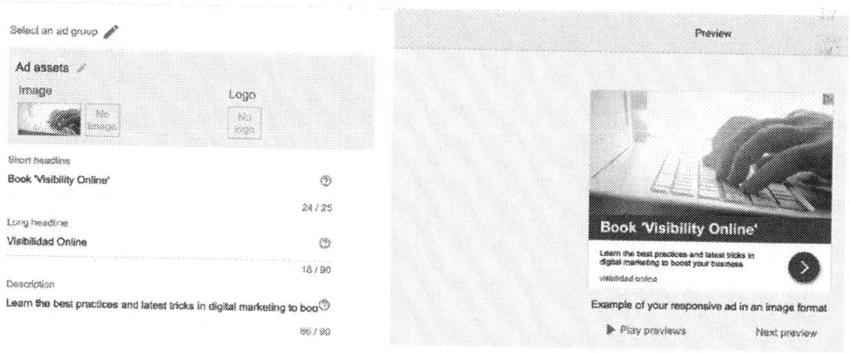

- **Image ads:** If you have graphic design skills or know someone to hire who has them, then you can place any elaborate visuals you need as per the example you saw previously from Adidas.
- **Ad gallery:** There are different templates which allow you to quickly create dynamic ads for Gmail and YouTube, among others, that will get more attention from visitors by having movement.

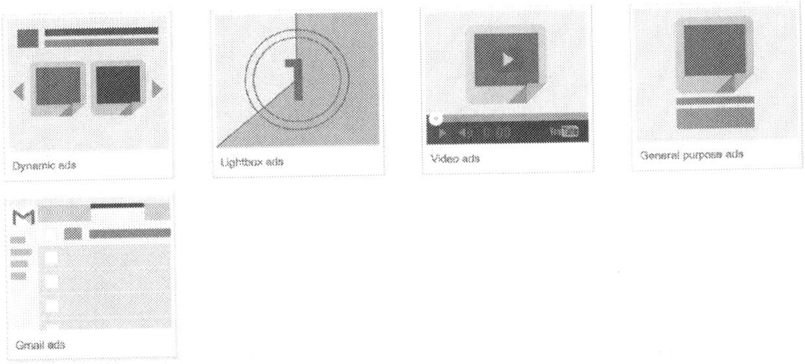

SET WHERE YOUR ADS WILL SHOW

With the campaign set up and the ads created, you'll only have to decide how, to whom and where you'll show your ads.

Create a new '+Targeting' and select one of the options described below.

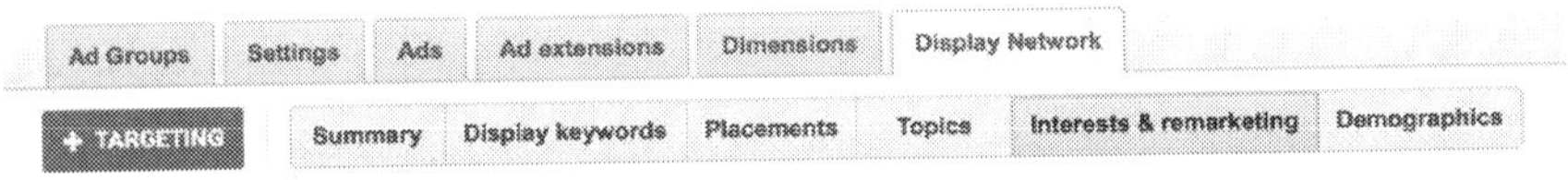

- Interests and remarketing: For finding audiences who are in your market and may have an affinity to your ads, you can suggest in which categories or interests your audience might be. Some examples are decoration, travel, DIY, sport, etc., and some categories have more specific sub-sections. Select the most relevant ones and you will quickly see the size of the volume of impressions you can get.
- Keywords: Often by selecting only very specific categories you may lose opportunities, but with the keywords you go can further, guiding Google as to which keywords you want to appear.

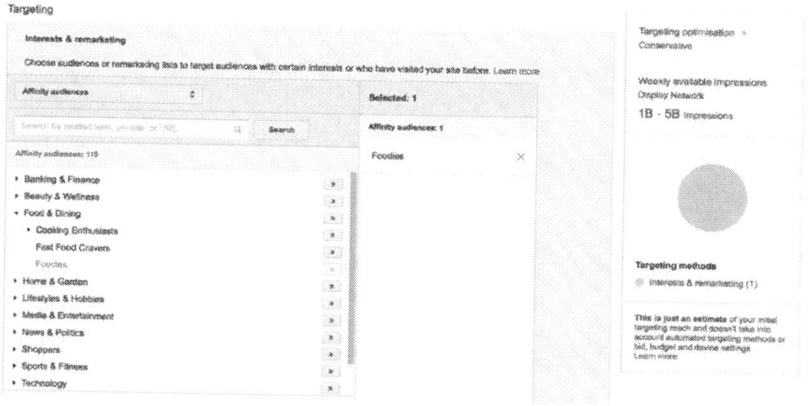

Imagine that you sell bicycles and in the categories targeting you did not select your ads to appears on websites about restaurants or hotels, but it turns out that a web guide of restaurants in your city publishes a blog about the route you could do on a Sunday with your bicycle, where to park it, etc. Maybe it would be a good place to show up, right? And if you have included bike-related keywords (and you have not excluded the restaurant category) then you will appear.

Go to the 'Keywords' tab and add the most relevant terms to give your ad a little more context, and make sure it's related to relevant content.

- Demographics: This configuration takes into account more the kinds of users who visit the sites your ad appears on, rather than the content of the site itself. Google AdWords and Analytics know a lot of information about users because many of us usually use their platforms (Google, Gmail, etc.) with our session open.

  With this configuration, you can focus on different age groups or gender. Very useful if your products are dedicated to the youngest who have the fastest adaptation to your new app or technology.

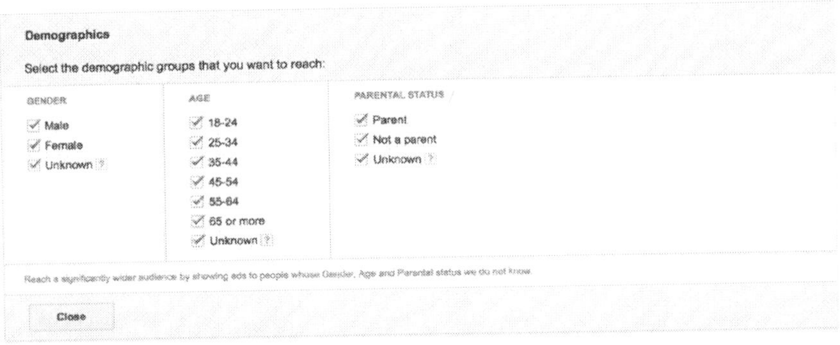

- Placements: Manually enter all the web URLs in which you want to appear. These can be at domain level or even specific pages within a site, if it has sections more relevant to your product.
- Themes: Unlike the category of audiences and interests described above, which focuses more on the data that Google knows about users, in *themes* you can select the context and content of the websites in which you want to appear. The example below is of a person interested in sports: the ad will be displayed on websites related to sports, no matter who visits them.

  If you have several of the settings mentioned above in the same ad group, they will act as an 'AND' condition. That is, your ad will only appear when both are met: if you have a keyword AND it's in a certain category.

Also, like the keywords in your search campaigns, these settings may be set as negative, meaning you may exclude particular categories, demographic groups, or websites, in order to make sure Google does not show your ad there.

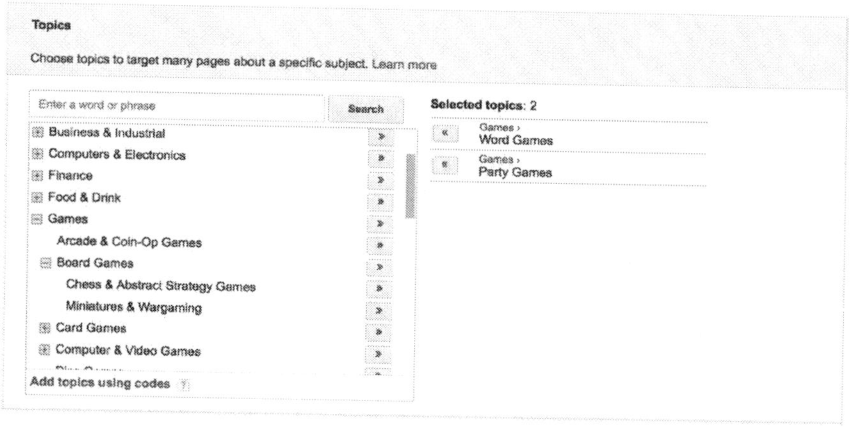
Topics
Choose topics to target many pages about a specific subject. Learn more
Enter a word or phrase
Search
Selected topics: 2
Games ›
Word Games
Games ›
Party Games
Business & Industrial
Computers & Electronics
Finance
Food & Drink
Games
Arcade & Coin-Op Games
Board Games
Chess & Abstract Strategy Games
Miniatures & Wargaming
Card Games
Computer & Video Games
Add topics using codes

25. ADS IN GMAIL

Gmail's advertising platform is very interesting for its option to show ads to all those users that have an email from a specific domain you are interested in. They can be your own emails, because you know that they are your customers and you want to sell them something else, or emails from your competitors or companies related to your service, so you assume that if they have received emails from airbnb.com, then if you are a hotel or hotel chain, you may very interested in reconquering those travellers who have found an alternative method to yours, so you can offer better deals.

Once you are familiar with Google AdWords, creating a campaign in Gmail is very simple. It's like creating a GDN (Google Display Network) campaign, but selecting a particular ad format. In the 'Ads' tab, click '+ Ad' to create a new one by selecting 'Ad gallery', and in the drop-down shown below it, select 'Gmail'.

Several templates that you can use will be displayed, some simpler with just an image or a piece of your own HTML code, or other formats with titles, descriptions and buttons.

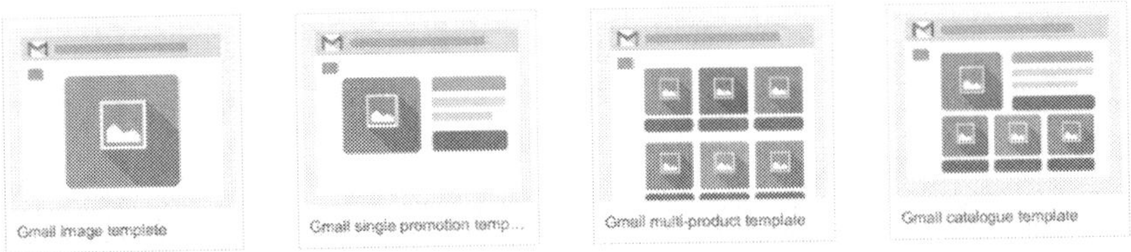

The example below shows the configuration for a Gmail advert for a fake restaurant named Bistro.

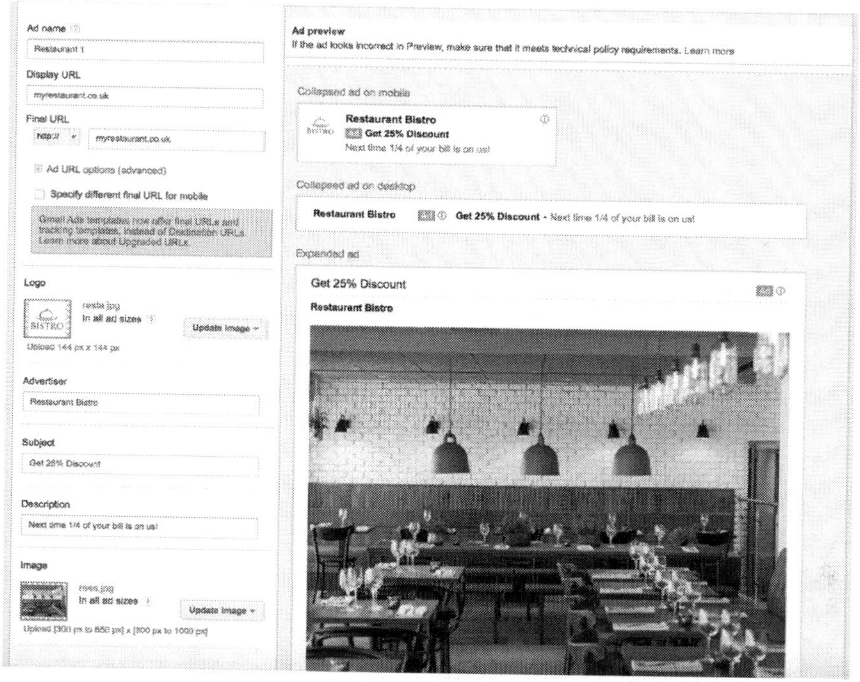

When users are in their Gmail account, they will see two promotional emails, and yours will appear as a 'Collapsed ad' as you can see above, with its small logo, title and description. Once the user clicks and shows interest, your complete ad will be expanded where you can inform them of your product without them having to go elsewhere to read more.

26. ADS IN YOUTUBE

YouTube is the second largest search engine in the world after Google. It is a fantastic channel if you are interested in promoting your video or advertising on top of videos with specific content relevant to your key audience. For example, if you sell kitchen products, you could choose to show your ad in videos about recipes.

YouTube is also very interesting if your goal is for the promotional video of your business to get greater exposure and more views, even if it is only for that purpose. I wouldn't recommend to invest in YouTube if your ultimate goal is for potential customers to land on a webpage to make a purchase, there are better and more direct channels to achieve that, like Google or Facebook.

YouTube works great to promote a new brand or product which could be difficult to explain with text or an image with only a few seconds of user's attention. That's when a well-crafted, quality, concise video with a very strategic first five seconds can really make a bigger impact.

There are different formats for advertising on YouTube. You can see the most updated list at:
https://support.google.com/youtube/answer/2467968?hl=en

The most popular format is the 'Bumper', which shows a video of at most 6 seconds before, during or after another video that users are watching and cannot skip. Also 'TrueView', where your entire video will be played, but with the option to skip after five seconds. If they skip, you do not pay.

To create an ad on YouTube, go to Google AdWords and create a new video campaign which will display a slightly different configuration than other kinds. Here the cost is not per click but per view (CPV), and the video formats you can choose will be shown in the next step.

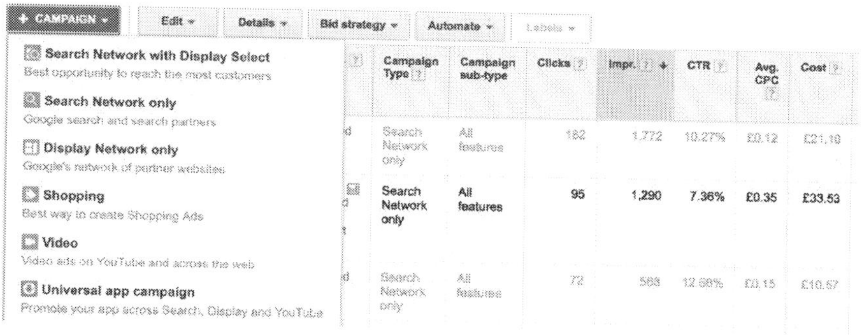

After you set up the campaign, you'll be prompted directly for what you need to create an ad, such as the YouTube video URL and the maximum bid to get views. But if you want to do it later or if you want to create a second ad using another of your videos, go to 'Ads' and '+Ad' by selecting the YouTube video you want to promote. You can search for it in the search bar or paste the URL of the video.

You can customise the look of your ad with different options by selecting a banner of your brand to accompany the video, as well as a friendlier address than the final URL of the landing page.

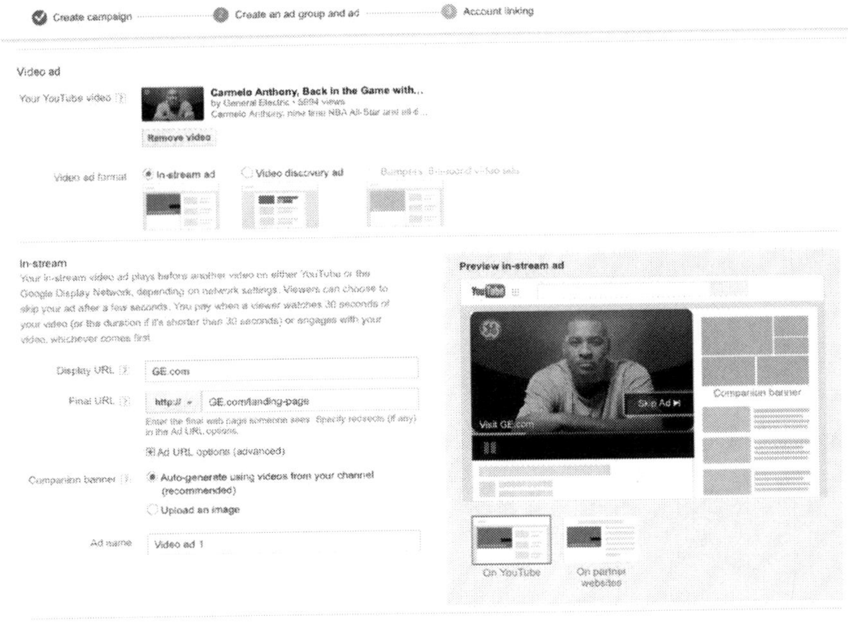
Create campaign
Create an ad group and ad
Account linking
Video ad
Your YouTube video
Carmelo Anthony, Back in the Game with...
Remove video
Video ad format
In-stream ad
Video discovery ad
In-stream
Your in-stream video ad plays before another video on either YouTube or the Google Display Network, depending on network settings. Viewers can choose to skip your ad after a few seconds. You pay when a viewer watches 30 seconds of your video (or the duration if it's shorter than 30 seconds) or engages with your video, whichever comes first.
Display URL
GE.com
Final URL
http://
GE.com/landing-page
Ad URL options (advanced)
Companion banner
Auto-generate using videos from your channel (recommended)
Upload an image
Ad name
Video ad 1
Preview in-stream ad
Companion banner
Skip Ad
Visit GE.com
On YouTube
On partner websites

27. ADS IN GOOGLE SHOPPING ADS - PLA'S

PLA is the acronym for Product Listing Ads. These ad variation is incredibly useful if you have an online store selling products.

PLAs consist of the results shown above the regular listings on Google when you search for a product that sells online through Ecommerce, which means that normal ads and organic results will already appear below them in a lower position, as shown in the following image:

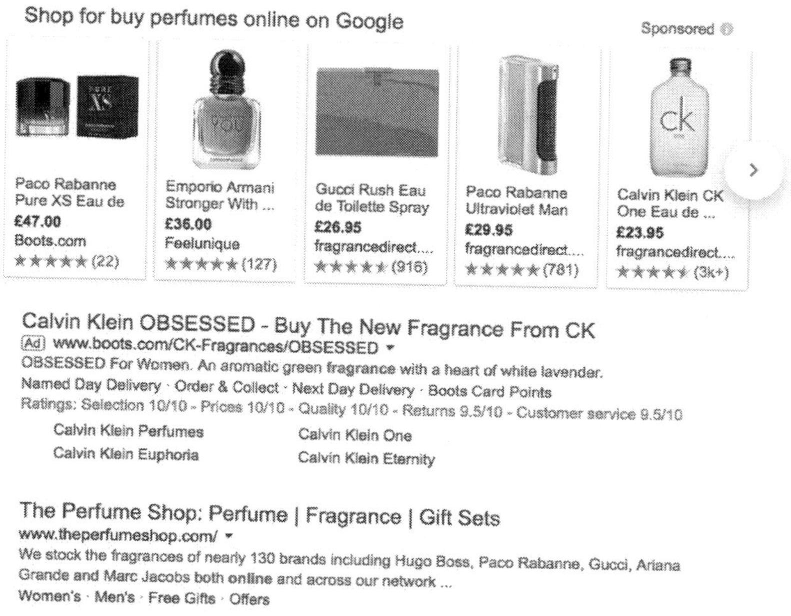

With *Shopping ads* in AdWords you will be able to show your product with its price, image, model and manufacturer along with similar products from the competition. Or in other words, it means you will also be there when your competitors sell online.

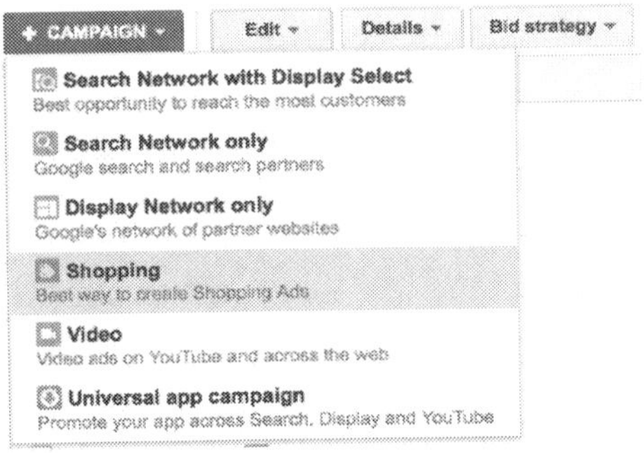

To create a campaign, go to Google AdWords, and from the 'Campaign' drop-down menu, select Shopping.

You'll be asked for a standard campaign setting, but the most important thing is that you have the AdWords account linked to another Google platform, where you'll have to create the inventory of all your products on sale: Google Merchant Center (GMC: https://www.google.com/retail/solutions/merchant-center/).

If you do not have an account created with your products yet, you will need to do this step first. Access to GMC and then sign up with the same Google account, and enter the information about your business requested.

Create your inventory by going to 'Feeds' and 'Add'. Note that you cannot create the products manually, but Google needs to have the GMC linked to something that can be updated online, like Google Sheets or another online platform. For example, use the WordPress plugin to link your WooCommerce inventory with GMC and transfer all the products automatically there.

If you have selected it through Google Sheets, GMC will create a spreadsheet with three tabs: the first one with all the information that GMC will read, such as ID, title, description, status, price, availability, image, etc. The second and third tab will help with instructions and examples so you can configure the spreadsheet accordingly. In short, though, when you have your inventory linked to GMC, and this with Google AdWords, it will suffice that you update the price or data in your original inventory management tool in order to see these changes come into effect in the final ads.

As this image shows, do not forget to go to the corner settings and select 'Account linking' so that the information is transferred to AdWords.

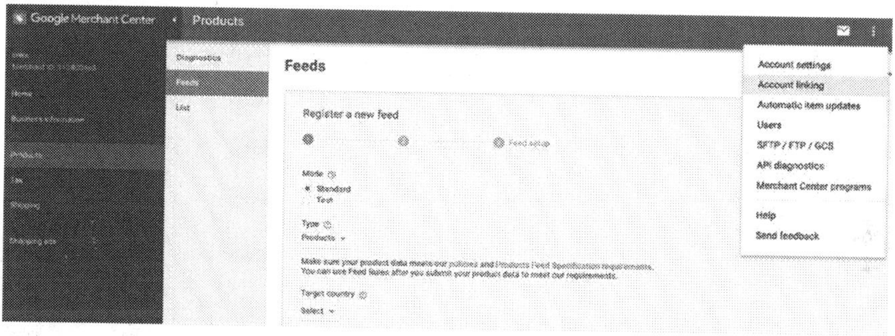

28. ADS IN FACEBOOK & INSTAGRAM

ADS IN FACEBOOK

Facebook can be a very powerful advertising tool and will become more so, since the American company has made very good moves in recent years to acquire a huge database of users through companies like Instagram and WhatsApp.

You have likely noticed that when you are looking at Facebook in your mobile application, many publications that are not from friends appear with a small writing that says 'Promotional', 'Suggested' or 'Sponsored'.

One of the biggest advantages of Facebook is its ability to advertise to people selected according to their tastes, gender, age, where they live, or to fans of similar pages or content in their publications. Soon they may be able to target according to user's private conversations in WhatsApp.

For example, if you sell perfumes online, you can make sure that your ad is shown to women aged 25-55 who like fashion, follow Vogue Facebook page and live in certain countries where you need a little help to reach your sales goal.

Your objective may also be to increase the number of fans on your Facebook page for future promotions, offers or other news that you usually share in it, so you can begin to reach more and more people organically with no additional cost. I would recommend to think twice about that goal, since if fans do not provide you income in the medium or long term through Facebook, you should be reconsidering whether it is worth investing a lot in that option in the first place.

Facebook campaigns are very effective if your audience is on mobile (90% of Facebook traffic comes from mobile), and obviously your website must also be adapted to different screens. In addition, it is perfect for promoting an app, because with only two clicks, users can be downloading one.

The cost of advertising on Facebook also varies according to whatever competition is targeting the same audience as you, and to the ad format you choose: Promoted news that will pass between your friends' posts is more expensive than the small ads on the right sidebar.

It is also very interesting to advertise in social networks if you have already done a previous job in them—that is, if you already have a certain number of followers or fans. who are already interested in your news, offers, promotions, images, etc.

With a good base of followers and fans you will get a bigger expansion to your promoted posts, since they will also reach even more users, and if they share a post on their timeline, you will be getting free promotion of your brand.

The latest studies reveal that users consume many more videos promoted on Facebook which have auto play and appear without volume, over the intrusive YouTube ads displayed before the video you actually want to see, where you have to wait some seconds to skip the ad. So I always think about Facebook for getting my videos to my audience. Consider adding subtitles to the videos for those who do not activate sound and watch in silence, since maybe your story without words does not transmit anything and you do not want to lose a user's precious seconds of attention.

ADS IN INSTAGRAM

The main thing you need to know about Instagram is that it is meant for mobile only. You can also view images from a computer, but without any other features.

Since Facebook acquired Instagram it has turned it into an ideal new platform for companies and their online advertising, and just like their blue sister, Instagram's main strategy is based on mobile.

If we think about why we follow brands on social networks, we will learn that it is often due to 'expectations'. We follow them because we know their usual content and what to expect from the next post, whether it is an image of food, a landscape, a customer wearing their clothes, etc.

The audience for Instagram is rather young, primarily because they were the first to adopt it in their day to day but increasingly, more and more older people use it.

Instagram offers a variety of very interesting advertising formats similar to those on Facebook, such as images with a link to your website or even videos that can significantly increase the ratio of interaction with the brand through comments or 'likes'.

One of my favourite formats, both on Facebook and Instagram, is the image carousel, as it allows telling a story as an image and then using it as a call to action.

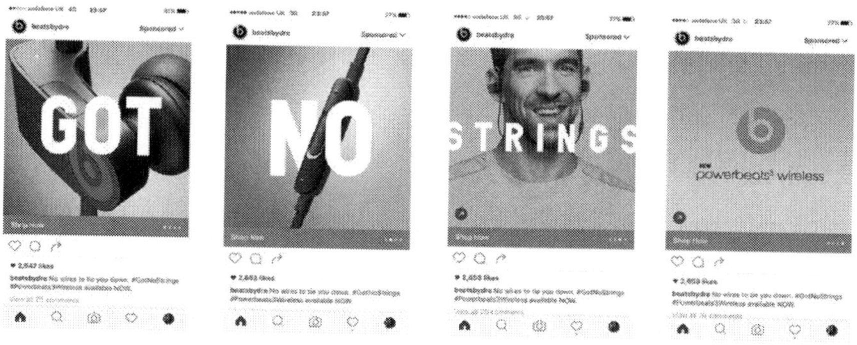

One mistake that brands often make when publishing images is to avoid showing the brand next to the product to avoid it being intrusive, but it is important to show the logo subtly or something that relates to the customer's subconscious, since otherwise you will have no impact on your potential client.

CREATE A CAMPAIGN IN FACEBOOK & INSTAGRAM

Facebook and Instagram, masters of user experience, are probably two of the simplest platforms on which to launch advertising campaigns for people with no marketing experience. You can do this by simply clicking on the 'Promote' button below each post on your Facebook page or Instagram profile, being able to spend a few euros as an investment, and making a basic selection of the demographics you want to reach. But here I will show you how to create more professional campaigns with more options.

To advertise in Facebook and Instagram you need to go to your Facebook desktop version and go to the configuration arrow on the upper right corner. Select 'Facebook Advertising' or 'Manage my ads' if you have already created them. Now, to the left of the interface you will see a navigating list and steps.

Select the objective of your campaign from the given options, according to the one that suits you best. Traffic is one of the most common, which consists of getting clicks to your website, but you can also target visibility (impressions), interactions (likes and comments), videos, or sales directly. Depending on what you choose, Facebook will ask you for further details.

Audience

In the *audience* section you can select the people you want to show your ad to, including country, age, gender, interests and whether you want to show your advertising to certain fans of other pages or with specific interests.

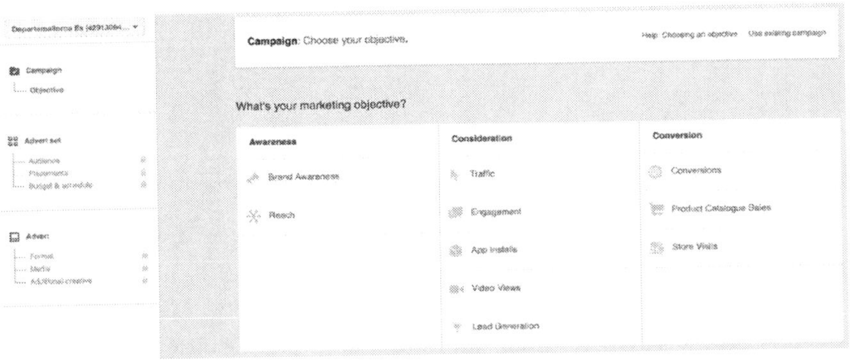

Placements

Configure what devices and areas within Facebook or Instagram you want to show your ad. I tend to focus on mobile devices, or when I target computers I usually exclude right column ads because they are much less effective and are easier to be identified as ads and not as camouflaged news.

Here is where you can also select Instagram to display image ads in that platform.

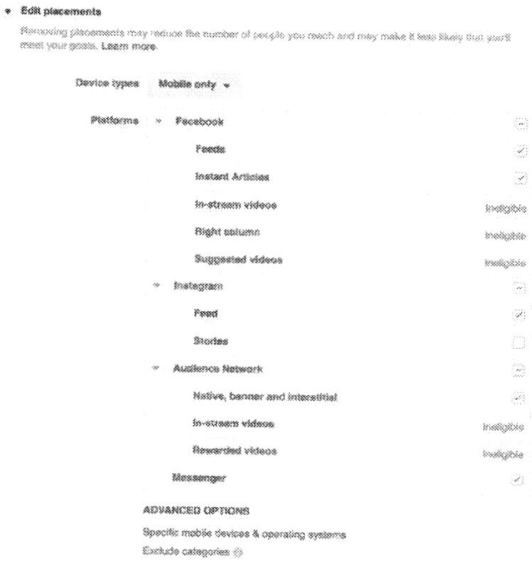

Ad

Facebook offers a wide variety of visual formats to capture the attention of your potential users. Think of the message you want to convey, and from the options provided, decide which one fits best with the images you have. Try different things and draw your own conclusions.

Set the budget and direction of traffic, and you're ready to launch your first campaign on Facebook. As you can see, it is much simpler and more intuitive than Google AdWords.

When you manage your ads, you'll get great detailed information about how they performed: when, where, who and how they interacted with your ad and page, so you can optimise your campaigns with this information.

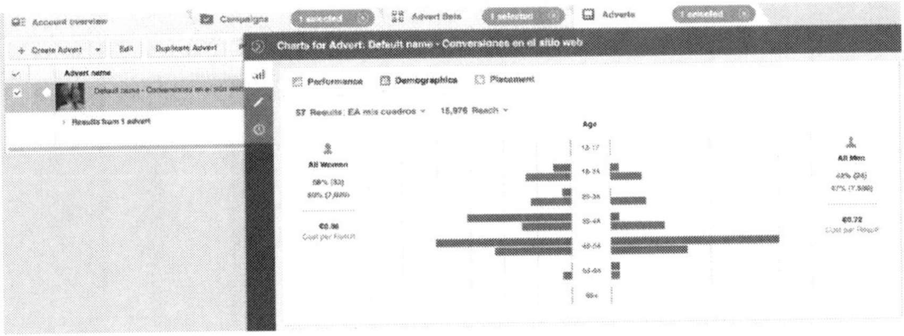

29. ADS IN TWITTER

The differentiator of Twitter with respect to other social networks is its importance in real time. Twitter advertising is ideal when you are interested in promoting tweets about events that are coming soon or happening, such as a conference at which your company will speak or introduce a new product.

Twitter probably has the least user reaction time compared to other platforms, as a 140-character tweet will disappear very fast from the users' screen (usually equivalent to scrolling down the screen of the mobile constantly with your finger). Therefore, the tweet should be the most relevant and with the most direct message you can convey.

There are also some formats that allow you to create a more complete form of advertisement, such as a web card, which includes a link and an image, and can capture more interest and click-trough rate. Twitter, like Facebook, is an ideal environment for users to download your app. In addition, the action button is 'Download Now'.

The segmentation you can make in this social network is interesting, because you can show your ad to followers of certain brands and competitors, people, and ultimately, any @handle.

CREATE A CAMPAIGN IN TWITTER

You can access your ad platform by accessing the drop-down menu above your profile photo. Click on 'Twitter ads' or go to ads.twitter.com and you will be presented with a menu like the one shown below, where you can quickly see the range of formats and choose the one that best fits your goals.

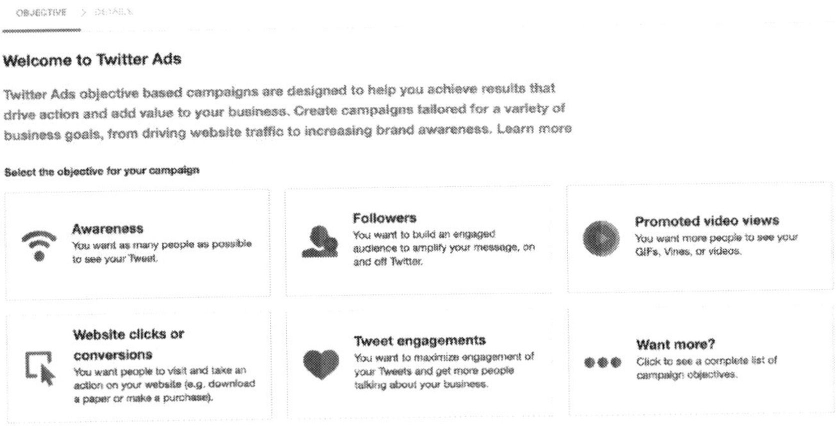

'Tweet engagements' is one of the most used formats on Twitter for generating visibility for your tweet, and for reaching a new audience that could be interested in what you say.

If, apart from visibility and creating a social conversation about something, you also expect them to visit your page, then the format 'Website clicks or conversions' will be more decisive, since you can incorporate a visual card showing some information on the site where they go, and you will occupy more space on the screen.

Whenever you tweet, either organically or for a paid promotion, try to insert an image and not only occupy the 140 letters, but to get extra real state.

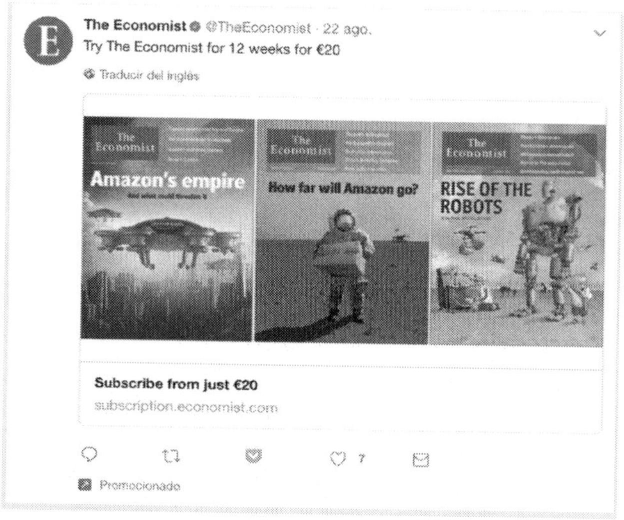

Another useful strategy, especially in the beginning where people do not know you, is to select the 'Followers' campaign objective. You will appear as a suggestion to the users that you select and you will improve your online reputation. Many people visit the social profiles of a company to know how many people trust it when buying or making contact.

Finally, if your purpose is to get downloads of an app, select the 'Want more?' option and 'App installs or re-engagements'. You have the advantage that users who see this advertising will already be on their mobile devices, so they will be able to go to the app store in a single click.

To set up who you show your ad to, Twitter allows you to select different targeting features such as keywords, account followers, interests, or even other elements very dependent on the element of time, which as I said before, is one of the strengths of this online channel—it allows you to relate your campaigns to events or television programs that often generate conversation.

30. ADS IN LINKEDIN

LinkedIn is the perfect medium if your main business audience is other companies or professionals in a specific industry. Unlike Facebook, here you can specify different configurations to show your ad to a much more professional and focused level of worker:

- Companies of a specific magnitude (by number of employees).
- Specific job titles such as directors, founders, C-level (CEO, CMO, CDO, etc.), who are generally the decision makers. But do not forget those who could also influence their decisions.
- Location and industry of the company.
- Fields of study, degree and skills among others.

The advertisement will be displayed to the user within the timeline, which is similar to other social networks in that you can add comments, share, follow the company or click on the link to head to a destination page.

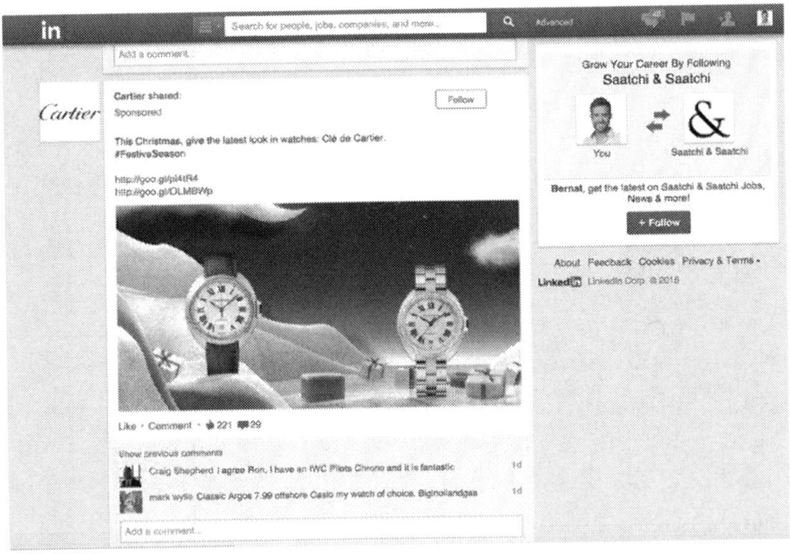

Starting a campaign on LinkedIn:

1. Create a profile on the professional social network for both you and your business.
2. You will see 'Business services' and 'Advertising' below the central search bar. You can also go to: https://business.LinkedIn.com/marketing-solutions
3. Select one of the three available formats and follow the configuration steps.

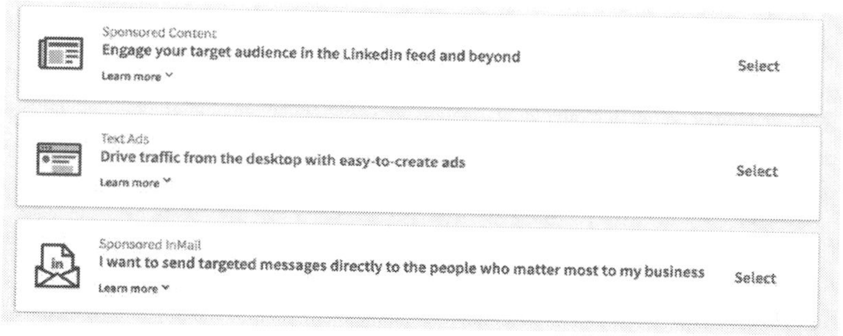

When you want to promote a piece of content or one of your LinkedIn publications through 'Sponsored content, you can select one of the existing ones in your business profile or create an new one without being published natively on your profile, also known as a 'dark post', by clicking on 'Create new sponsored content' and writing the new text and image you want to publish and show to your audience.

Once you have created the campaign, you must select your target audience. And as I told you before, here comes the strength of this platform. You can select employees of specific companies, size, location, skills and seniority, among other options.

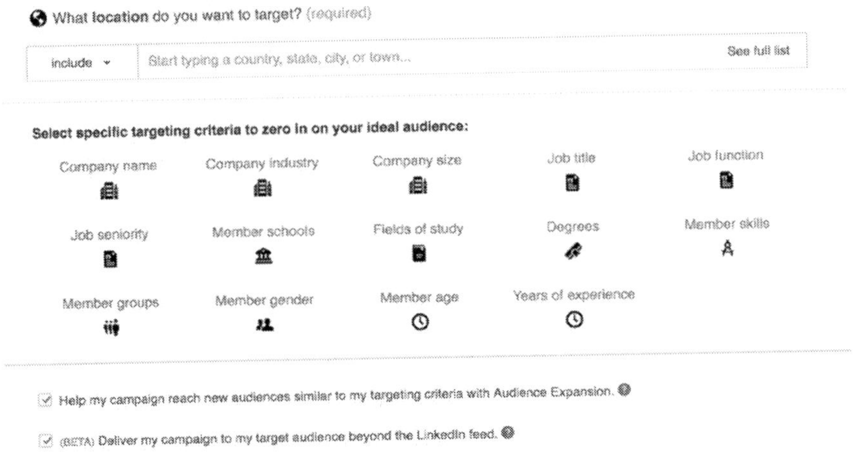

One of the powerful formats recently released is InMail, which allows you to send a more elaborate, personal and long message to your audience with a call to action at the end. It is a useful option when you are not so much after traffic to your website but instead want to get your message to your potential customers. Examples of its value are for promoting an event or course, news about one of your products, and for limited offers.

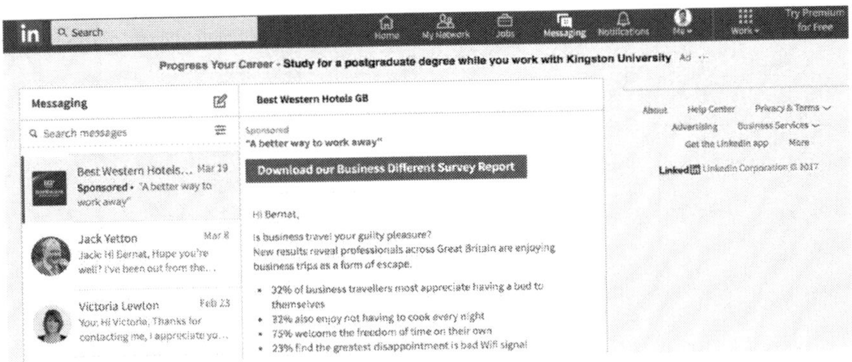

31. RETARGET YOUR PREVIOUS VISITS

I'm sure you've visited a travel website or online store, and subsequently, you have seen their ads across other websites, even specific ads related to the trip you searched for. That's called remarketing. This system is based on cookies and consists of setting a cookie for all those users who land on your website or go to a certain page of your site.

You can create a segmentation of users who have previously visited your site and they may be potential customers, because they either know your brand or have been interested in your products at some point (e.g. they searched Google for a keyword and ended up on your site, or viewed and clicked on one of your Facebook posts).

REMARKETING IN GOOGLE SEARCH – RLSA

Search remarketing consists of showing personalised ads to those users who search again for one of your keywords once they have already visited you and been tagged with your site's cookies. Perhaps, on the first visit, they did not have time to complete the purchase, or maybe the product that you showed them was too expensive or not relevant enough.

But they have searched again, so here you have a second chance to get their business. In order to do so you must carefully determine your strategy and what you are going to say now. In this case, you could include even more generic keywords, because you already know that they are a potential customer from their previous search and you have a smaller margin of error.

For example:

- Show a cheaper or alternative product

If you sell printers and you showed an advert of an expensive model the first time this user searched for 'laser printers', and they left without buying it, now that they are looking again, do not show them the same printer, but a lower model to see if the price was the problem. Or, if you did not previously specify black and white or colour in the advert, consider showing the alternative this time.

- Offer a discount

In your new ad, show a temporary promotional discount to get their attention, and a short-term opportunity to take advantage of that offer.

- Personalise the ad

You can also improve your message to these repeat users by trying to show your value against the competition, as they obviously are interested and are researching the market for their best option.

To set up these campaigns, you have nothing more to do than create an ad group of the ads following this strategy, and once you have the keywords you want (which may be even more generic than you would use in a normal group), add a new segmentation from the 'Audiences' tab by selecting the remarketing list you want and the 'Targeting and bidding' option, which means your ads will only show to your selected audience looking for those words, not to any other person that searches.

How to create a remarketing audience in Google AdWords

To create a remarketing campaign in AdWords you will first have to create an audience, and there are several methods of doing this, such as through Google AdWords or Google Analytics. I prefer the latter, but just in case you're not familiar with Analytics, I will also show you how to do it in AdWords.

To create an audience in Google AdWords:

- Go to 'Shared Library' / 'Audiences' in the vertical menu on the left.
- Create a new remarketing list according to what suits you best. The most common option is 'Website Visitors'.

- You can also select options like users who have visited a certain page, or people who visited but did not end with a conversion.
- Go back to your campaigns and select the ad group to which you want to assign an audience. Select 'Interests & remarketing' tab, create a new '+Targeting' / 'Interests & remarketing' / 'Remarketing lists'.
- Select the desired remarketing list.

How to create and export an audience from Google Analytics

Here I will have to assume that you already have Google Analytics platform running and tracking your website's traffic. You can refer ahead to Phase 6 to see more information about Analytics.

In Google Analytics, you can handle all the traffic that your website receives no matter where it comes from (e.g. paid, organic, social). And once you've collected the right data there, you can start grouping and segmenting that traffic as you want. You can then import this back to Google AdWords and serve them the ads you want.

Select who your potential customers are, divide and conquer. Here I will show you some examples of the audiences that I have created from the traffic of esglaiart.es, to demonstrate our advertising strategies for potential clients and artists:

- Men between 35 - 60 years old who have not registered before. Statistically, we know that men interact better with an online art gallery, and selecting from age 35+, we are focusing on those who may have more experience of painting, and may imagine that their work is of a higher quality.
- Another group that we wanted to show advertising to was those who had found us by a source other than Google–like Facebook or Twitter–so the next time they search for something related to the art world in Google, we will show our ad and hopefully they will recognise the brand and click.

Creating an Audience in Google Analytics:

1. Audiences, like goals, are created from the 'Admin' main menu at the 'property' level.
2. Click on 'Remarketing' to create a new audience.
3. Generate your audience by applying the filters you want, as explained above.

Or a simpler way: create a 'view' in Google Analytics, selecting the conditions you want, and use that view to remarket them. For example, I have added a segment with the traffic that bounced—in other words, those who arrived on my page and left immediately.

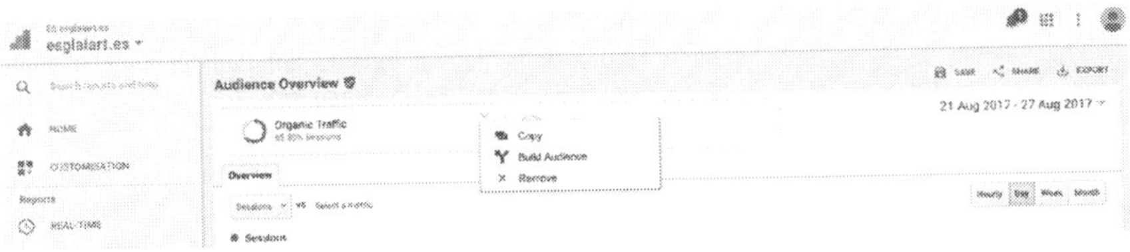

Then select with the 'Create audience' menu, and you will jump directly to the management tab and audiences with that option selected.

Make sure you have AdWords linked so that this audience can be imported from the advertising interface. You can also link AdWords with Analytics at 'property' level.

Then in AdWords, you just have to apply the new audience to your ad group using the method I described earlier.

REMARKETING IN GOOGLE DISPLAY NETWORK (GDN)

A more common and less elaborate way of doing remarketing is by displaying banners or text ads on different web pages belonging to the Google Display Network (GDN).

Visits to your website will set a cookie for users, allowing Google to follow them and show them your banner, again reminding them at different times or on different days about your product or service, and trying to call their attention to completing the purchase or request.

It is important to limit how often these users see your ad every day, as it could become intrusive and annoying, causing a negative influence on your brand.

REMARKETING WITH GOOGLE TO VISITS FROM OTHER NETWORKS LIKE LINKEDIN OR FACEBOOK

This strategy is very appealing if your customers are companies (B2B - business to business), since LinkedIn will allow you to find employees in specific companies or industries who would be very difficult to identify by their searches on Google.

For example, if you are the manager of a hospital and you search in Google for 'generator', you are thinking of something very powerful and expensive for your hospital and your purchase journey will be much longer compared to a mountaineer looking for for the same word 'generator', which probably will be interested in something much smaller and lower power. How can we differentiate that 'generator' search? With LinkedIn.

Through LinkedIn you can target your potential customers by identifying where they work, such as hotels, hospitals, factories, companies with more than 50,000 employees, staff from a specific location, and other options. So if that director of hospital that clicked on your ad in LinkedIn, got your cookie, went to Google and for 'generator', then you know it's him and not the mountaineer.

Alternatively, it might be very valuable to target the audience that has come to your website through social networks like Facebook, Instagram or Twitter, and you found them because they have certain interests as a fans of certain music or online games and you want to sell them a new console.

STEP 5

USABILITY AND USER EXPERIENCE

32. WHAT ARE USABILITY AND USER EXPERIENCE?

Usually confusing, but usability and user experience have different meanings. The first is a quality attribute on the ease of use of a web to achieve certain objectives and the second covers much more than that, encompasses the emotions, feelings and, in general, the 'experience' that a user has or feels when interacting with your business, which will go beyond the web browsing, but until they buy a product, receive it and use it, in addition to their interaction with your sales team or technical support.

The usability and experience that users have in our website is not universal for everyone, as each person will be different and you will have to create a design as best as possible so that the experience of most of your potential customers is the best they can have.

It is known as web usability to the discipline in charge of studying the way in which the design and operation of a web page is related, and the possibility that the user can use it comfortably, easily and intuitively.

To achieve this, the premise that should not be left out is trying to achieve a design that focuses on the user, that is, create according to what others want or expect from the site. This goes against what many do wrong by presenting designs that are too complex and often only understood by the developer or programmer.

Improving usability makes us focus on the interaction of visitors to complete the tasks we want them to do, such as buying the quickest and most intuitive way by eliminating blockages and simplifying processes.

On the other hand, the UX or User Experience, refers to how a person feels when using a particular product, device, or in this case, a website. It is the emotional connection with your business, application or web. Usability is only a layer that impacts the entire user experience.

It is the value they get when using it. These can get all the information they need on your website and be about to become a customer, but when you call your sales team you realise that the offers are not applicable in the small print, which causes a feeling of rage which could generate a negative word of mouth for your business.

It will be very important to understand how your brand is perceived by users so that you can improve it and achieve success with your products. For this you should not be afraid to ask the opinion of your customers. If they are negative, you should know as soon as possible.

Returning to the design of your web page; the web designer or programmer should never underestimate the users' skill or ability to choose to use one web before another. The more time passes, the more able the users are to distinguish between what is a good experience on a site and what is not.

To have a successful UX you have to understand:

- Who are your users or potential customers online?
- What they will want to get on your website.
- What will make them tick the box "I'm happy"?

33. FEATURES OF A GOOD WEB EXPERIENCE

It is easy to learn

Learning is synonymous with the first time, and this is what you have to keep in mind about the simple learning of your web. How easy do users have to complete a specific task on your website for the first time?

To give you two examples, one positive and one negative, remember how easy it is to make a hotel reservation on www.booking.com for the first time without ever having done it, since it is very intuitive and guides you through the whole process so that you do not even ask yourself what's next for you to do.

Instead, when I wanted to unsubscribe from amazon.com, I went to the web and it was very difficult to find it (I understand that it is on purpose), but not finding it I returned to Google to redefine the search ('cancel account in amazon') and see if their direct results helped me to reach my desired destination. It was not intuitive at all.

Easy to remember

A user may have used bank accounts online before, but he has not accessed it for some time and maybe the look has changed, or he has become accustomed to using his second bank. So how easy would it be to remember to operate on the first one?

Even if you update the web to improve usability, try to leave clues for those users who have already learned how to use your page.

User's performance

The goal is to perform a specific task, which could be from asking for an appointment to visit your physic business until a direct purchase online. Ask yourself how effective and fast a user is by performing those key tasks for you. Ask your friends to do them in front of you.

Try to make it as fast as possible and with the fewest errors. Clear the way and make your interaction intuitive, efficient, and proof of misunderstandings or mistakes.

If we have to explain to the user how to complete the task, then it means that it is not well designed, and you can not be with all the visits explaining it to each one. Every second saved is an improvement on the experience.

Improve visual design

- Pre-set recommendations

Many of the excesses that are committed during the planning and design of a web happen to avoid copying others or want to demonstrate originality almost to the point of rebellion.

Do not hesitate to follow patterns already established by others: The clarity of the titles, information well distributed in space, the best places to put images and the best combinations of colours in case you have different categories of information so that these are well differentiated from each other.

- Adaptability of resolution

The way in which the information is distributed, the sizes of the designs, the presentation of the web, in general, must be able to adapt to different devices and resolutions. Users not only use the site from computers, but nowadays you will have more visits from mobile or even from smart watches, virtual reality systems and smart assistants in the home. The typography you use has to be large and clear on any device.

Simplicity

Many focus their efforts on creating visually striking sites or worry too much about aesthetics and minimal detail. Most of the time, less is more.

The idea is to avoid complex designs, and give preference to flat figures that avoid the user's cognitive effort. Of course, this does not mean that beauty and visual impact are not important, but the main thing is to avoid excesses.

Simplification is a basic element to improve usability over any other recommendation. Note that Apple products have the minimum number of buttons. Google only has one bar to enter words. Our web pages are full of words, links, images and actions.

USER JOURNEY MAPPING

Meet the users

For this it is good to conduct studies before and also after the launch of the website. This will help to have clear information about what users expect and the experience they had then on your site. Social networks facilitate this path and are a great ally in knowing the perception they have about our service and if their needs have been met.

Intuitive Thinking

This is a key aspect to take into account when establishing the options, functions and way of arranging the information in a website. The attention span of users is often limited, and often oriented towards cognitive laziness. For this reason, actions that require a lot of effort on the side of the user or complex designs that make him tired should be avoided.

INFORMATION ARCHITECTURE

Ease of navigation

Your website should make things easy for the user, this point is key among all the criteria of web usability. It prevents the user from having to make too many clicks to access essential parts of the site, much less have to make many more clicks to return to the beginning or Home.

A website where browsing is poor will be a scared-clients site, and this is what every business or business wants to evade. Avoid keeping broken links inside the site, or cause confusion in the user while browsing the site. Too many plugins can cause slowness and deficiency while browsing the website. It is necessary to choose the ones that are really necessary.

THE CONTENT AND ATTENTION OF THE USER

Minimalism

It is an artistic trend that minimises your means of expression. Faced with this trend, it is necessary that on our website design style avoid all unnecessary and irrelevant elements such as colours, textures and shapes. It is about focusing the user's attention on the content, avoiding it being distracted with other elements or colours of the web.

Designs that direct attention

There are certain design features that will allow us to guide users to wherever we want in any content or action. These are in order:

- Movement: Any dynamic element on a page will catch the eye of the beholder. Putting a quality video (although light) on the home page as background can be very catchy. You will also see that the format that most advertisers on websites use are dynamic banners with animations or movements.
- Size: The greater an element, the more it will stand out compared to the rest.
- Colour: The human eye is only able to highlight or appreciate 5 different colours at a glance, so avoid overloading the page with too much variety and maintain a certain tone and general theme in your design. The elements that break with that dynamics will stand out, so be clever using them.

- Orientation: We are accustomed to seeing objects aligned in horizontal lines. If there are elements that break with that orientation they will draw attention to the observer.
- Location and position: The items above the fold will obviously be most viewed and noticeable for users so also take into account when positioning key actions or visuals to increase the conversion.

34. HOME PAGE DESIGN

You have one chance to capture the interest of the visitor. Critical first impression and experience to judge your brand, company and offering. Also known as the home page.

The home page is the only one allowed to get out of the default design of the rest of your pages, and you have to be able to show visitors what the web looks like in a nice and attractive design.

If your website represents a cooking course centre, you should be able to print out your home page in paper, show it for 5 seconds to 10 people and ask them what it is. If one of them tells you it was a restaurant, it means you have to change the home page.

Get an immediate image in the head of everything you should find in it. You have to prevent the user from wondering if there is this or if there is the other, or where it is. So, following the example above, if I go to the home page of the cooking course centre, I should be able to see what categories of recipes they have, what city they are in and a calendar of courses (or at least a simple notification that says: "The next course starts on 25 of May, sign up now "). With that note I would know that there are courses, that I can join the next, and that I can find out their prices. I do not want to think, give it to me quickly and with one click away.

Before you start creating pages, menus and widgets, take paper and pen and design how you want the general structure of your page to be. In it, visualise where your goal is, where you will make money, and make sure that all roads lead to Rome.

If you want to increase the number of clients, make sure that on each page where you explain your services, blog posts and home page have a call to action at the bottom of the page as a great exit door from that content.

If your goal is to sell products, the user has to find what they are looking for easily, so you must put filters so they can get closer to a potential product and thus prevent them from leaving the site without buying it.

Titles and their relevance have to be highly identifiable. Do not waste space with a welcome message. Remember that in a paragraph of text, the useful thing competes with the useless when it is read by a user in 10 seconds.

A good trick to see if your web is easily readable is if your content could be read aloud and fast. In addition, if your page meets that, you are already ahead of the new techniques of web browsing and search engine positioning: Could Siri or Alexa read your website while driving?

NAVIGATION AND MENU

The menu will play an important role for users to find quickly and intuitively what they are looking for. Try to sort from left to right where your pages are, from major to minor from an economic point of view.

The structure of your content should be represented in the menu. In addition, to help users navigate and let them know where they are at all times, it is very useful to place a breadcrumbs on each page by means of small links, allowing the user to see what level of page he is in and how to jump to another category if they were not where they wanted. For example, imagine a user landing on this page after clicking your result on Google:

Cycling> Bikes> Folding Bikes> Raleigh Evo-2

At a glance, you already know that you are on a folding bike page (you can understand that there are also normal ones) and that it is under bikes (so there will be other things under cycling *Nutrition*) and currently looking at the Raleigh Evo model.

If you want to compare other folding bikes and filter by price or location, you know that you will click on 'Folding Bikes' and see the full catalogue. And if you might consider buying a new normal bike, then go to the all bikes clicking to "Bikes".

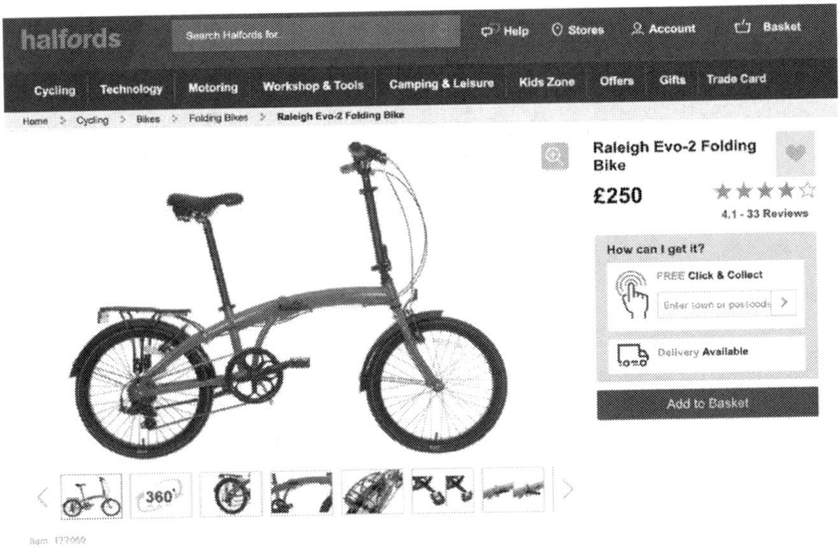

35. USABILITY FOR ONLINE STORES

IMAGES AND STORE LAYOUT

Assuming that your products are of interest, you have competitive prices and people arrive at your website, the few seconds you will have to definitively catch your customers or send them away to your competitors are the images of your products. It is even more important to invest in a good photographer than in a web designer.

Images have to have the highest resolution possible, but looking for a balance with the weight of the file, since the large files will slow down the loading of the page.

Many objects lose their perspective on images and it is difficult to appreciate their size, so I recommend that when you can, put another object commonly known. For example, if you sell porcelain vases, you could show them on a pretty table next to a pencil. Being next to the pencil you can already have a quick idea of the dimensions of the vase.

If you sell clothes and in the images you show a model, I also recommend putting a small legend about the size that the model uses. In this way you can see if the style of the shirt that has a wide cut in itself even if it takes the size small, or help any other perception that each can have on sizes or styles.

The images should be as large as possible and with the possibility of zooming well defined to observe the details.

Some have the option to rotate them 360º, although their photography and processing is more complex. Nowadays, thanks to an internet so fast, we already see many product pages with videos as well as still images.

Finally, whenever the product allows you, show it in its pure state, in use. If you sell hiker backpacks, show a man taking it up a mountain and having a great experience with it, with which you can identify yourself and increase your desire to purchase.

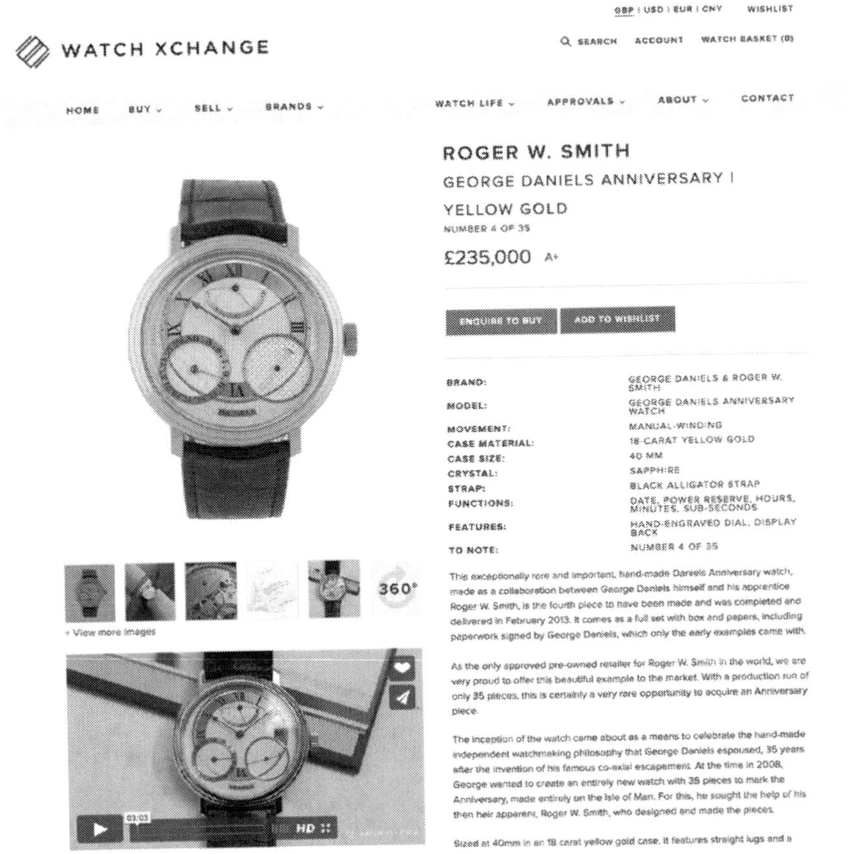

IMPROVE THE SALES RATIO OF YOUR STORE

Once you create your store and start receiving visitors, you'll have to optimise it to increase the conversion ratio through the different tools I've shown you, but I'll also comment on a couple of specifications about selling more in online stores:

- Be obvious with what is sold in your store and let clear contact information visible.

- Displays reviews of other users. Recent Google research shows that 70% of online shoppers only complete their purchase after they have read several customer's review.
- Add credit card logos like Visa, MasterCard or PayPal and accredited online store certificates (you can get these logos by registering at: trustonline.com). With these, users know immediately that the products or services there are paid and not for free.
- Product Descriptions: Try to write original and useful content on the product and best in bullet points format.
- Keep a personal tone with your visitors and customers consistently across your pages.
- It is mandatory that your ecommerce has good navigation from the mobile, both to find the desired product until the purchase confirmation.
- If it is handmade or unique products of some kind like clothing or art, do not hesitate to display images of that added value with the craftsmen creating them.
- Reduce distrust to customers: clearly shows the warranty, the period of return with its cost, etc.
- Add widgets from Facebook or other social networks where you show the number of 'Likes' or fans of your page.
- It offers different shipping options, with different delivery times and prices.
- Have fast access categories for repeating visitors, such as 'New', 'Best sellers' or 'On sale.'
- If you sell things that can be given away, give the gift option in which the product will be wrapped to be sent to the final recipient.
- Add an internal search engine and make sure it delivers the results you are running.

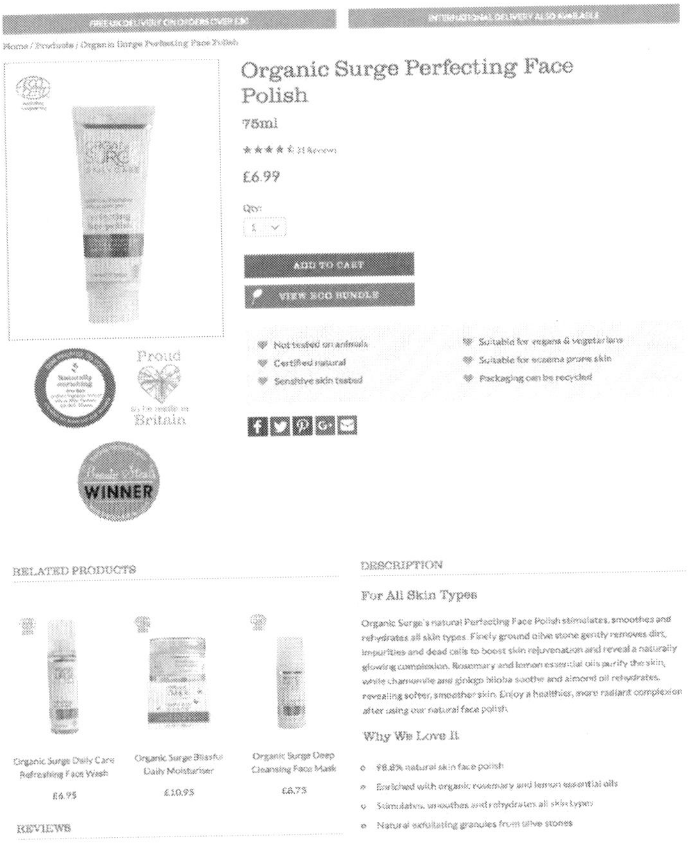

- Recommend products related to the one to be bought, such as packs or products that are usually bought together.
- Reduce the number of clicks until the end of the purchase.
- Add a pop-up plugin to detect that the user is about to leave (when the mouse moves to the top of the browser). Try capturing their email to send future offers or give them a discount code so they don't go away yet and you can push them to complete the purchase.
- Set up some automatic basket recovery system. If customers left the store leaving products in the basket, you have an opportunity to remind them via email that they have those products to buy,

so you remind them that they do not have to do everything again but these are ready for them to buy them.

- Finally, collect feedback from customers who did not finish their buying process. Try to find out what went wrong or which page has the highest bounce rate through Google Analytics.

36. TOOLS TO IMPROVE AND ANALYSE USABILITY

The only way to know if your users are interacting as you expect with your portal is by asking them.

I have to say, my opinion does not matter. Neither of the others. I may like my website a lot, but it does not really matter. You may like my website a lot, but if you do not buy or convert on it, it does not matter either.

Your website has to be, be seen and used in the way that brings you the most business, regardless of your success metric (sales, contacts, downloads, navigation, interactions, etc.) and for the greatest number of possible users.

So there is no secret formula or help guide. The only and best thing you can do is test different versions of your site to analyse how different users behave in one compared to the other, and find out which one suits you best. Then you keep the winning version and compare it again with another.

A/B TESTING

When doing an A/B experiment, the following pages are usually called:

Page A - Original (or control): It is the page as you have it by default, the one you originally designed and you think is the best.

Page B - Experiment or version of A: This is the version that will compete with the original page.

What to change in variation B?

- Single change per test

There are many books that talk about old school AB testing, which recommends changing a single element of the entire page and seeing how that change affects it. For example, change the colour of the 'Reserve Now' button from green to orange.

The theory of this way of experimenting is that you can control exactly what improves or worsens the conversion ratio, because if you make several changes at once, for example, if in addition to changing the colour of the button you change the background image and the order of the navigation menu, you will not know what caused the greatest positive effect or the one that influenced negatively.

- A completely redesigned page

I'm not so optimistic when I test. I do not like to assume that my initial design is so good that with minor alterations I can get big changes. Perhaps I'll be able to improve my website by reaching its peak conversion ratio, but who says that redesigning another version of the site would not double the results in less time?

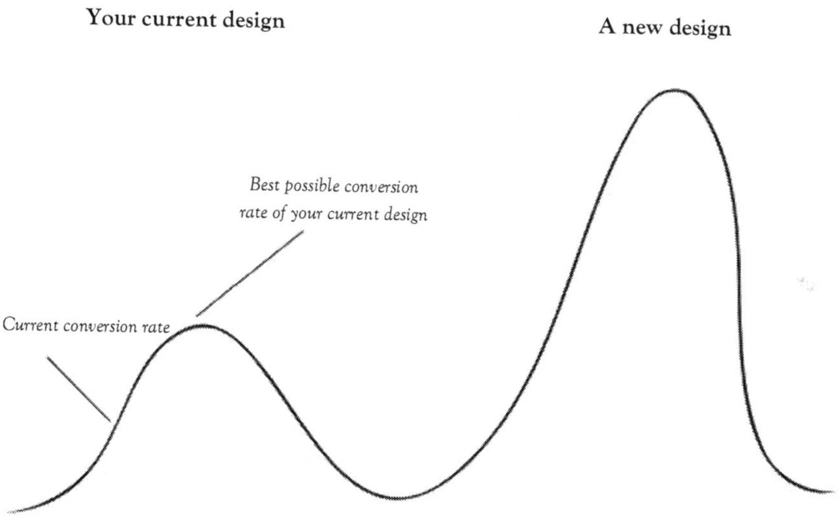

Indeed, one of the best techniques to come up closer to the ideal website or landing page would be by sticking bigger jumps and getting much more progress from blow.

Consider to optimise a single page rather than the whole website, as that would take much longer. You have to focus on the page where you want to improve your goal, and every page can have a different goal.

For example, on the home page, your goal may be for people to end up in the store. But in the store, your objective is that they buy more shoes than complements, since they give greater margin. Then, on the individual product page, your goal may be to click more on the buy button.

These following tools can help you to get closer to your high performing landing page:

TOOL # 1: OPTIMIZELY (AB TEST)

Optimizely was initially developed in the campaign of Barack Obama to raise funds for the campaign, and this tool caused an optimization of the visits and donations received daily. Due to its success, the application was further developed. It was free for many years, but now you only have 30 free trial days that could be very useful depending on the volume you receive per month. There are also free tools, but I will focus on explaining this because it is the best in the market and its cost can mean great benefits.

It's very simple to use and I'll explain how. You do not need to know how to program HTML, CSS, or anything like that. It has no relationship with your WordPress.

1. Sign up: Open a free account on www.optimizely.com
2. Create a project by clicking 'New project' / 'Web project', from the hamburger menu on the left corner.
3. Go to the 'Settings' and get the code that you are to paste in the header of your web, just after the <head> tag, at the top.

4. Create an experiment (for example, 'google move button), which will belong to that project (google test) and where you will group all the tests or variations you make to the particular page.

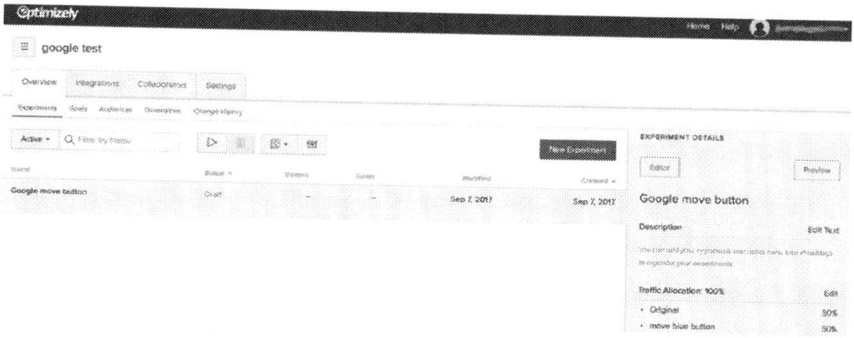

5. Access 'Editor' to see the control panel of your experiments. Note that you have a tab that says 'Original', and subsequent tabs you can create by clicking on '+' to add Variations.
6. Create a variation and you will see how now your original page is copied, but which can be modified very easily by clicking on the different elements of the page. In this example below, I selected the 'sign up' button from Google and select *move and resize* to easily drop it near the main logo.

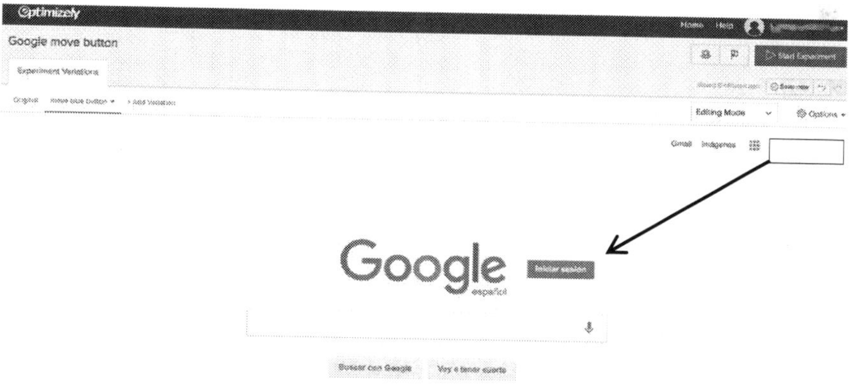

The possibilities of editing depend on your programming skills, because if you are good at it, you can do anything by manually editing the HTML code on the spot, but if not, you can modify many other things intuitively:

- Modify the colour of the text, its message, its background colour, its size, relative position, border, etc.
- Move place items on the page. With a simple click and drag you can place any button or text in any coordinate of the screen.
- Change images either from a URL or from a file on your computer, which will upload the image to the Optimizely server, so you do not have to worry about the space or its storage.
- Create links on any word or phrase of the content.
- Resize any item.
- Delete objects as the same navigation menu, preventing users from going to another page.

You can also set goals when users perform certain action by clicking on elements of your web as buttons or links, and 'Track Clicks' as goal.

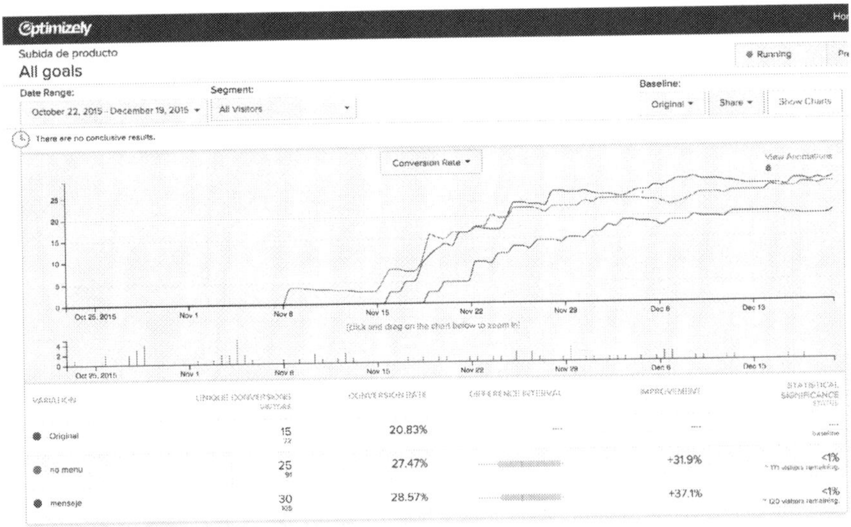

In the results of each experiment you can analyse how your changes are impacting the conversion ratio or total number of goals, among other metrics.

The previous visual example (an A / B / C test) shows how the conversion ratio improves over time, and during that experiment period the variation without menu presented an improvement of 31.9%, and the change of message in the page tested showed an increase of 37.1%. Although it is essential to have enough traffic so that statistically it can be affirmed that this variation is the winner.

In addition, in the configuration you can establish how much of all traffic received on the web will be tested (80%) and the original version (20%). After the 80% sent to the test, you can distribute the traffic in a non-linear way as in the example, with only 40% of the 80% sent to the variations. This is very useful when you want to take less risk and receive a lot of traffic.

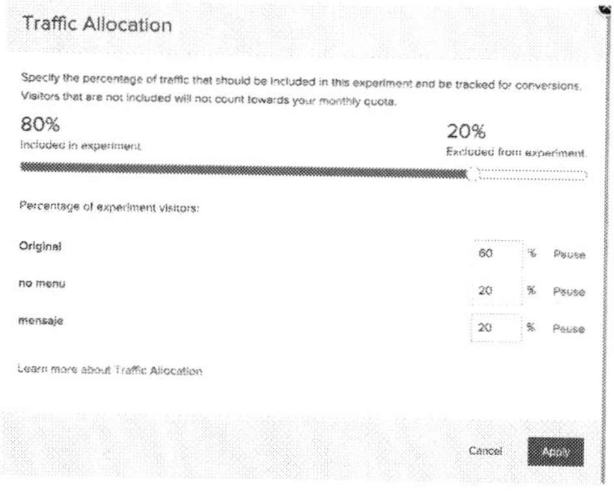

TOOL # 2: USABILITYHUB.COM (ASKING COMMUNITIES FOR FEEDBACK)

The key portal to ask questions about your site to other usability experts. It is cheap and as a community allows you to propose tests to other users, as well as you provide your opinion to their tests.

To create a test, you first have to buy credits that will get you as many answers as credits you have. There are 4 types of tests:

Click test

Users will see your question and a screenshot of the page you want to test. They can click once or several times, depending on your choice.

Common questions are: "Where would you click to register on this website?" Or "Click on all places that you think would lead you to pay this product."

Once you get the answers you will receive your screenshot with a heat map of all the points you have clicked and the average response time indicating that the longer they take, the less clear it is. Additionally, you can also know the demographic data of users who have done the test, such as their ages, nationalities or gender.

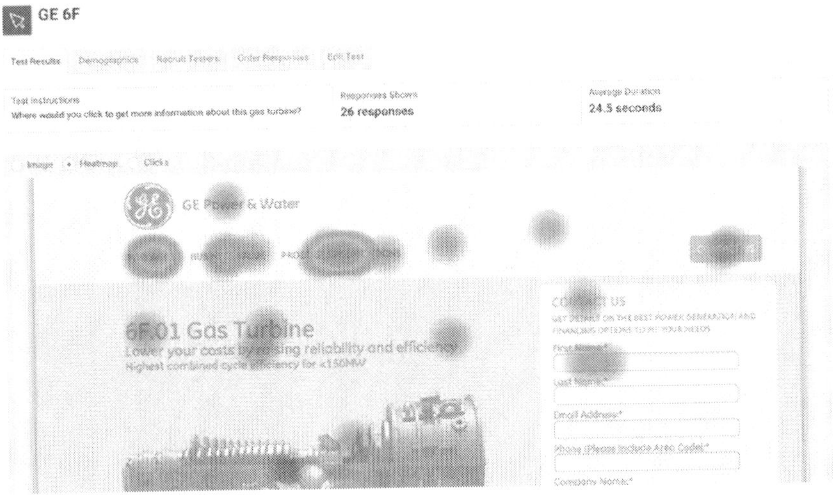

Five Seconds

This test consists of showing your page to users for 5 seconds and then the image will disappear. The user receives certain questions about that image, which will allow you to find out if the purpose of your page was clear enough and if within 5 seconds they understood what your page was about.

This time is usually the decision lapse in which a user decides whether to stay on your page or go back to the results to find a better one. You can ask several things, like "What service did this website offer?", "What was the brand of the company?".

Preference test: Show 2 images side by side with a question on top of them, and users will have to click on a single option. This test will help you decide when you are in for a couple of ideas. For example, "Which design do you like best?" Or "Which website do you find most intuitive?", "Modern?".

You can use this test to compare and ask what you want, for example, two titles on a page, or two Google ads to see which attracts the most attention. I used it to get more opinions about different possible cover designs for this book:

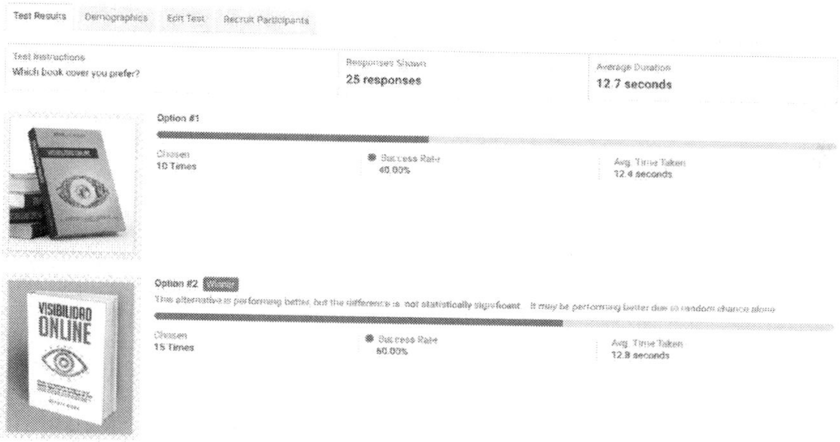

Navigation test

With this test you can ask the users different steps to reach a goal, and you can see if they follow the expected path or not.

The navigation will be composed of images so that even if they are wrong on your first click, you will see the second image you have prepared and clicking on a position again, the third image will appear. If nobody fails in navigation is that your design is perfectly intuitive.

TOOL # 3: USERTESTING.COM (VIDEO USAGE RECORDINGS)

When you are developing the final design and you are about to launch your page, stop for a second and do the following. Look for users around you (as long as they meet the requirements of potential users of your website) and ask them to access to your URL and do a specific task.

I imagine you will ask them to do something with which you would benefit from your real customers. These tasks could be:

- Enter the web and make a reservation for Tuesday at 7pm.
- Buy the size 42 red Nike shoes.
- Download the latest podcast available.
- Try to send me an email.

Although you don't believe me now, I'm telling you from experience that users will not see it as easy as you. With one of my first designs for a second-hand directory website I asked some friends to upload an ad while I recorded how they did it.

My design had an upper menu with uppercase letters that read "PUBLISH YOUR AD", but nobody saw it! They went to contact, FAQs, footer links, etc. The income came for uploading paid listings on my site and nobody could easily find it how to do it!

Ask people of different ages, sexes and professions. When you see a common pattern in all of them, change the web to make it easier. Once the change is made, look for a different audience and repeat the process.

There are portals like www.usertesting.com, with which you can get videos from users around the world using your web to detect problems.

You can assign them a task, and following your written instructions on what you want them to do, you will get a recording of their computer screen, even with audio with them walking you through, where they explain what they are looking for and doing at any moment.

TOOL # 4: CLICKTALE OR MOUSEFLOW (HEAT MAPS)

Another solution that complements the other tools is the analysis of heat maps, which shows you how different shades, from blue to red, how most of the mouse pointers have moved on a particular page, as well as viewing where they have been clicking.

It is very useful to detect the main route of the eyes of your users when they land in your web design and which links are the most predominant in the menu, or if the images of the content distract or serve your main objective.

With more complete systems you will be able to analyse in which step the users leave a registration form, since perhaps it has too many fields or there is a specific one that represents a problem and many end up leaving it.

There are different options in the market that allow you this analysis, from free like Google Analytics, to more specific and complete products such as Clicktale or Mouseflow. Most of these software have a cost, but using their 30-day trial versions already allow you to start getting an idea.

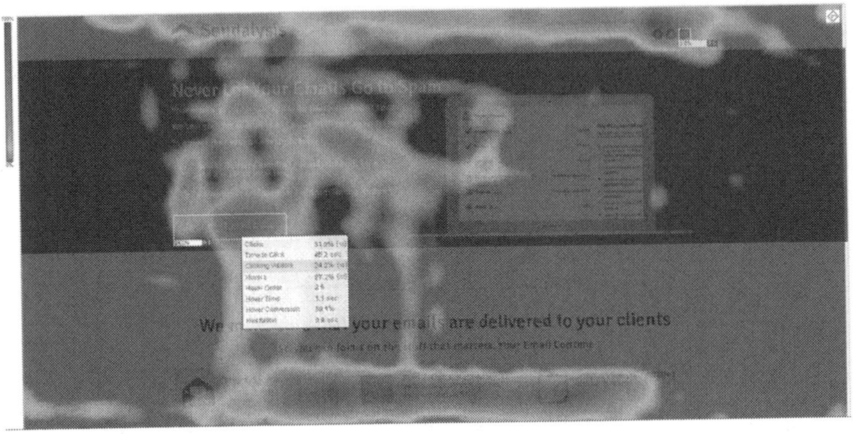
are delivered to your clients

STEP 6

ANALYSIS AND MEASUREMENT

37. GOOGLE ANALYTICS: ANALYSIS OF YOUR WEB TRAFFIC

The number 1 analysis tool, full, free and with Google's reliability. I could write a whole book about the different analysis we can do and the detailed information we can obtain; so I will do the same thing as I did with similar complex chapters: to focus on the important things, give you the guidelines on how to navigate, and which information you should analyse and understand in order to make the best decisions that could improve your final results.

To start Google Analytics, you will need to have a Google account and go to google.com/analytics. If you already created one for Gmail, Google AdWords, YouTube or other Google services, you will log into Analytics right away with one click.

WEB PROPERTY STRUCTURE AND HIERARCHIES ON GOOGLE ANALYTICS

You could be tracking several websites under the same account. To add one, click on property and 'create new property' and insert the URL.

You will be asked for an account name and a property name. I will explain what they mean in a moment. They are not definitive, so you can always edit them through the Admin panel.

The different levels define the grouping of websites and their analytic reports, as well as the different features and configuration that you can set at each of the levels. These are:

Account

It is the highest level on the scale. If you had different websites for different clients that you have visibility of, then here, you could create an account for each group of websites/client. The configuration at this level allows you to grant access to other users of all the accounts under that property.

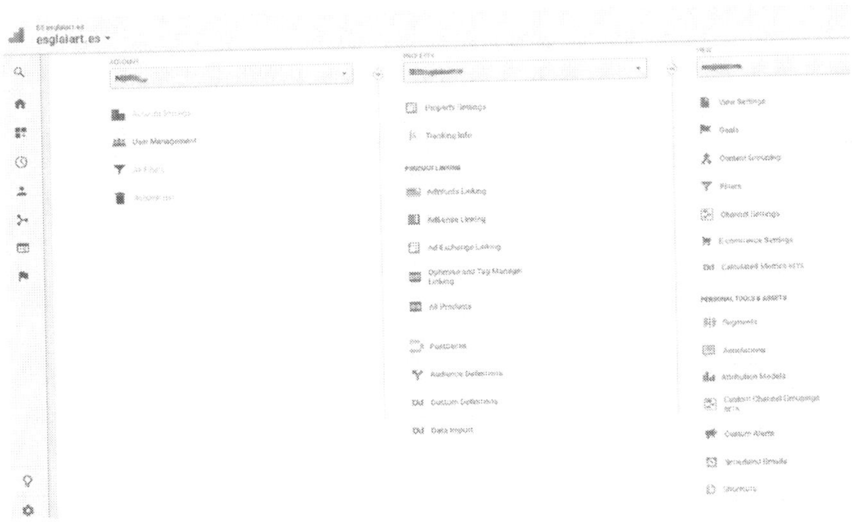

Property

It is one of the most important levels, since you should have one property per domain, subdomain or app. Google Analytics will generate a code for each property that you add with a unique identifier which code will be placed in the header of the specified domain.

The piece of code will be generated through the 'Tracking Info' section. Remember that a subdomain is a different web from the main domain, so if you have apple.com and store.apple.com, you need to have two properties with two codes generated.

It will also be at this level where you will be allowed to link Analytics with other Google products such as Google AdSense, Search Console or AdWords, very easily if everything is under the same Gmail address.

Finally, here you can find a very interesting feature for your online paid campaigns which is to create audiences for your 'Remarketing' strategies. I will expand more on audiences later on in this section.

View

For each property, you will get a default report view, although you can create many others.

For example, you could have a lot of traffic on certain pages, and you would want to view their traffic statistics directly, such as your website's store (mydomain.com/store) or blog (mydomain.com/blog).

So, under the ownership of mydomain.com, you would have three views: the home page (mydomain.com), the store (mydomain.com/store) and the blog (mydomain.com/blog).

In addition, in views, you can include reports already filtered by default with the information you want to see. Not only a specific page as in the previous example but also to see data from a certain source of traffic such as organic or Facebook.

Many times, the name given by default, both at this level and in property, is not the most intuitive one when you have to search on the web, but this is easily editable by going to the 'settings' section in its respective column.

At the view level, you also set the 'Goals', which will be the identifier of success for your traffic. In this section, you will set what you consider a conversion or goal accomplished. Some examples that you could set are:

- View a specific page. Each time users go to a certain page, which could be the 'thank you' page after completing a purchase or completing a request through a contact form (http://mydomain.com/completepurchase), it will count as one goal accomplished.
- A certain user behaviour. You could consider a goal is accomplished if users spend more than two minutes on your

website browsing or reading. Or browsing through more than three pages.

- By events. Follow the clicks that happen at certain points on the website, such as a button to download a PDF file or an image. To follow these events, it will be necessary to configure a small piece of code in the buttons or links.

ACCESS LEVELS FOR OTHER USERS

At all previous levels, you can configure the users who have access to them and their rights. These are inherited downwards; for example, if you have an account-level editing permission, you also have it in its properties and views. The types of permit levels are:

- Admin: This is the permission that will allow you to grant or revoke access to other users. This permission does not include other level rights such as editing or collaboration, so you will select them independently and complementary.
- Edit: Access that allows you to manage and work with all the repot-related functions, such as adding accounts, properties, goals, linking other products like AdWords, etc. It includes the 'collaboration' permissions as well.
- Collaboration: To collaborate on shared elements, edit a panel or annotation. Includes reading access.
- Reading and analysis: To see the data of the analysis only without being able to collaborate or edit anything else.

SETTING UP THE GOOGLE ANALYTICS CODE IN YOUR SITE

From the first moment you launch your website, make sure you have the Google Analytics tool perfectly integrated for the right monitoring of your website's performance.

You can get the code from the property level, accessing to

'Tracking Info', you will access the panel that will show you a code like the one below:

```
<script>
 (function(i,s,o,g,r,a,m){i['GoogleAnalyticsObject']=r;i[r]=i[r]||function(){
 (i[r].q=i[r].q||[]).push(arguments)},i[r].l=1*new Date();a=s.createElement(o),
 m=s.getElementsByTagName(o)[0];a.async=1;a.src=g;m.parentNode.insertBefore(a,m)
 })(window,document,'script','//www.google-analytics.com/analytics.js','ga');
 ga('create', 'UA-22Y37X91-1', 'auto');
 ga('send', 'pageview');
</script>
```

The code has to be placed on every page of your website, and to do that, it is best to place it in an element that is across all the pages which are either the header or the footer.

Header and Footer are also two specific PHP files on your website that you need to open and paste the code. To find the header.php file in your web folders, you must access via FTP to your website's directory and find the header that is in the template of your web. Note that, you will have a file called header.php in each of the template folders you have in your WordPress (and brings some per default); so you should locate and paste the code in the directory where your current active template is. For example:

```
/wp-content/themes/myactivetheme/header.php.
```

Then, paste those lines before the header is closed with its closing tag </head>.

You also have easier options. You can download and install the 'Header and Footer' free plugin for WordPress, which allows you to easily place codes in those areas.

MAIN METRICS ON GOOGLE ANALYTICS

From the home page (or report tab), you will access the main performance panel showing the most relevant metrics as a summary for a certain period of time, which you will be able to change by selecting the time range you prefer from the calendar in the upper right corner.

In the main report, the most relevant analysis metrics for online traffic are already shown, although all information can be much more granular with the following filters and sections. It is important to recognise the main ones and what they determine:

Sessions: The total number of times your users have visited your web. Here, the number of unique users who have landed is ignored, so if the same person accesses 100 times to your page, 100 sessions will be counted.

Users: Represents only people who have accessed. Following the example above, only one visitor would be counted. For me, it is one of the most important values of my web traffic since it tells me how many new people I reach each week through my efforts in positioning, social networks or advertising campaigns.

Page visits: It sums up the total number of interactions with all pages by any users across all their sessions.

Percentage of new sessions: Shows the ratio of new users visiting your website out of the total and obviously, you can get the % of the ones repeating, so those who already knows you. Getting new users is great, but the repeating ones are also important because it means that you offer them value every time they come back, as well as being in their minds when they have to buy again something you offer.

Ideally, both new and returning users should increase over time. But, it is difficult to indicate a benchmark percentage since it will depend on your goal: If you are interested in showing products from your website to new people, then a successful ratio would be about 70% of new visitors vs. 30% of returning visitors. But, if your online business is focused on a niche sector or based on trust and recognition of your brand, where users consume your content on a regular basis, then you are interested in reaching more people for as long as possible and keep your audience loyal and engaged.

Pages/Session: When you are trying to improve user navigation and reduce the bounce rate percentage, it is very useful to check this parameter knowing that if they only look at one or two pages, you should help them to keep going through links and information until they end on your conversion target page, i.e. your store.

Bounce rate percentage: represents the number of visitors leaving the web when they have just landed, either by going back to the search results where they came from or by closing the page without navigating.

The lower this percentage is, the better. If it is high, you should understand that visitors or users are not finding what they are looking for directly on your home page. And so does Google. If a user searches on Google, clicks on your result and seconds later, goes back to search for a better result, it seems that Google did its function wrongly, so the next time another user searches for the same thing, Google will show your link some positions below and try to improve that experience for the user. And you don't want that to happen if the search was actually relevant for your business.

NAVIGATION AND FILTERING ON GOOGLE ANALYTICS

On the left panel, you will see several differentiated and large analysis groups:

Real Time

The 'real time' section will show you all the visitors who are, at that moment, on your website. It can be very useful to analyse the launching of a campaign that you want to follow closely or to compare the traffic at a certain moment when you are broadcasting your company's advertisement or other advertising such as a radio ad.

You will get detailed information about the location and visitor' overall number, even by seconds!

Audience

It is the place to find all the details at user level. In the 'Overview' sub-tab, you will get a data summary panel, but you can always dig deeper by displaying others such as:

Demographics: Gender of your users and where they are. Very useful to perhaps discover who your best audience are, for example, men between 35 to 55 years old and from 5 specific states from the USA, so that you can focus on them in your next advertising campaign.

Technology and Mobile: Browsers and devices, which your users navigate from. I recommend that you identify the most relevant and used ones to test how your page is displayed on them and how their experience is when browsing. You can use real devices if you have them or go to websites that offer simulators of all devices and browsers, such as browserstack.com.

Acquisition

Following from the previous point, about where users arrive from, the 'Acquisition' report will give you information about the different traffic channels, such as:

Direct: Users who directly enter your domain URL into the browser. With this, you can measure the number of customers who are faithful to your brand and will go to your content directly. Many of them will have it saved to their favourites or bookmarks in Google Chrome, or it also means your URL is easy to remember and no need to Google it.

Analysing the trend of this traffic allows you to evaluate the loyalty or recognition of your brand over time, or to detect a traffic spike when you have done some offline campaign like appearing in a local newspaper. In that way, you can see, for instance, how on that specific day that the ad went printed, you had a 30% increase in direct traffic from those who have manually entered the URL, and assuming they have seen it on the pages of the newspaper.

- Organic

Visits received from organic and free search results. Probably most of them are from Google, but you can find out if other search engines like Bing or Yahoo have also participated.

In addition, if you have Google Analytics linked to the Google Search Console, you'll be able to get details on the organic position, and exact searched words that directed the traffic to your website. You will find more details about this source of traffic in the 'Search Console' sub-tab.

- Paid

The payment report will reflect those visits that come from advertising campaigns. These can be from any platform, such as Google AdWords, Display banners on websites, advertising on Facebook, among others.

If you are also in charge of these AdWords campaigns, I recommend linking Analytics with AdWords and going to the 'AdWords' sub-tab to link all the visits and their metrics to your campaigns, keywords, and cost.

- Social

Tracking all the traffic coming from social networks like Facebook, Instagram, Pinterest, Twitter, among others.

- Referral

Referral visits from other websites through their links to your site. And, as I mentioned in the SEO section, this is a very important traffic because it tells Google how many websites out there are talking about you. And the more influence you have in your industry, the bigger that traffic from other websites will be.

Referred traffic does not include other sources already considered in other categories such as social or search engines.

Use UTM codes to track customised Medium and Source

You can add some universal parameters (or UTM codes) appended at the end of all your URLs that bring traffic to your website and are under your control which means you can edit them, such as advertising campaigns, without altering the final content of your website. There are several parameters, although the most used are the campaign (utm_campaign), source (utm_source), medium or channel (utm_medium) parameters.

UTMs are intertwined regardless of the order through the '&' symbol, and they are all attached to the original URL by the '?' symbol. For instance:

```
http://miweb.es/restaurante/menu?utm_campaign=Ads-xmas&utm_source=Facebook&utm_medium=red-ad-mobile
```

These codes or tags that are placed to the URL will also appear in our Google Analytics reports as 'All traffic' / 'Source / Medium' tab, indicating all the traffic they have generated with their individual statistics.

Although you can set these parameters to whatever you want, I would recommend you to be constant in your assignment throughout the different channels.

Google provides a tool to generate these codes easily by just entering the parameters you want. Visit:

https://support.google.com/analytics/answer/1033867?hl=es

and go all the way down, where it shows you the fields where you can enter your website, campaign, etc. And after you have completed it, click on 'Generate'.

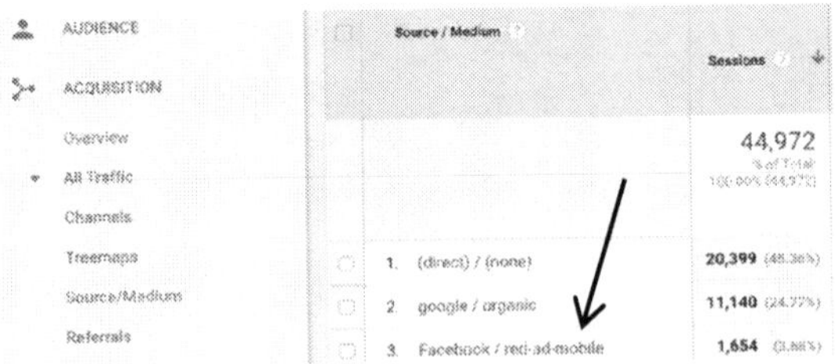

Copy and paste that address where it belongs. In my previous example, that URL will go on the advertising campaign URLs I prepared for Christmas and specifically for Facebook, on the ads that will be displayed on mobile phones with a red background for my identification.

Besides these, you can set others like utm_term, utm_keyword, utm_content, etc.

Behaviour

Behaviour Flow: A very interesting graphic will display the flow of the traffic across your site. It detects which pages are the most visited and where visitors go after them.

On the other hand, it identifies the page where the largest exit rate occurs, so you can try to optimise those pages to reduce it.

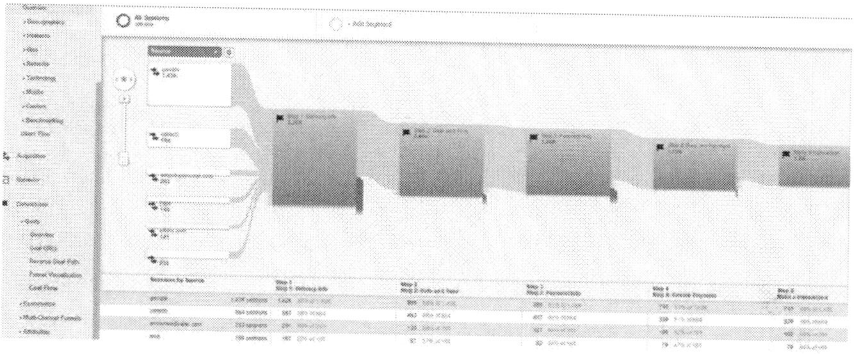

The top filters will allow you to choose the starting point of the analysis, for instance, from a particular geographic location, or through a specific channel where they arrived from.

You will see if, depending on the case, your landing page varies, or if the navigation behaviour is different depending on whether users have found you through organic results, paid campaigns, knowing the brand and accessing the web directly or from social networks.

On the left-hand side navigation under 'Behaviour', you can find one of the most important analysis regarding the navigation of users through your web, which consists of individual statistics for each page or different URL. You can see a full report and filter the list of all the URLs with the search box to obtain the total number of visits in a certain period, bounce rate, etc.

For example, if I want to know how many visits the gallery with paintings and all traffic to the individual paintings are getting, I can filter them on the search bar by '/paintings/.

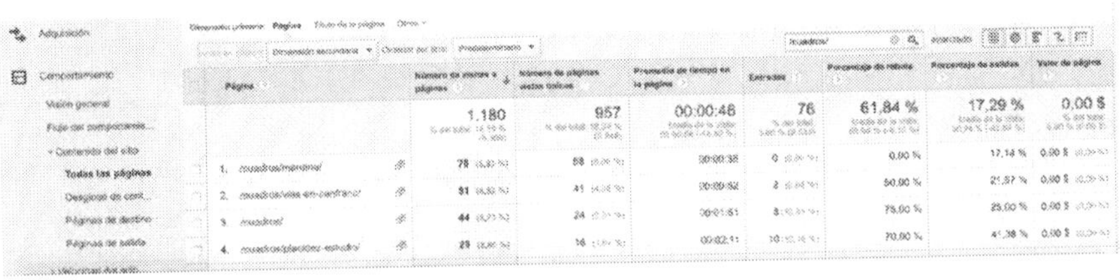

Speed

It indicates the average page load time, which gives you an individual reference at the page level and helps you to detect certain elements that can take longer than average to fully load, perhaps due to large images or amount of content. When you detect the slowest pages with Analytics, then take them to be analysed deeper with other tools such as Pingdom (https://tools.pingdom.com/) that breaks down the times for each element of the page to identify and optimise (or replace) the slowest.

Goals

To obtain data in this section; first, you will have to configure the goals from the administration panel, selecting the property and view that you want, followed by 'Goals'.

For me, it is one of the basic elements of our analysis, and it is where I spend most of the time because this is where you will measure the success of your traffic and all your online campaigns. If you only analyse visits, but you are not sure about what you want to get from them, your SEO or SEM campaigns will not prove to work, as well as your hours spent publishing on social networks.

Decide what has to happen on your website, so we consider that you are succeeding. These goals can be:

- Visits to certain pages from the website, such as contact, request an appointment or a quote.
- Sell a product
- Time on site or on certain pages
- Money generated through advertising

Once created, you'll be able to analyse when, how, who and where these conversions occur, as well as which channels are involved in generating new conversions, among others.

'Funnel visualization', 'assisted conversions', or 'conversion paths 'will give you meaningful information to understand in more detail how well or poorly your ad campaigns or other channels are working. Who helps to generate more conversions? SEO to paid ads, or vice versa?

Many people invest in display advertising (web banners) to increase brand awareness, and some days or weeks later, those users who clicked on the banner, go and search for your brand to finally click and convert, which means that Google' search will take all the credit for the good performance, but the display banner also helped on the journey.

Although from my experience, a lot of times the opposite happens: Users search, investigate and leave, but they come back days later when they see a banner on a website as a reminder (remarketing). So, the display advertising would be successful in this case if the attribution was given to the last click.

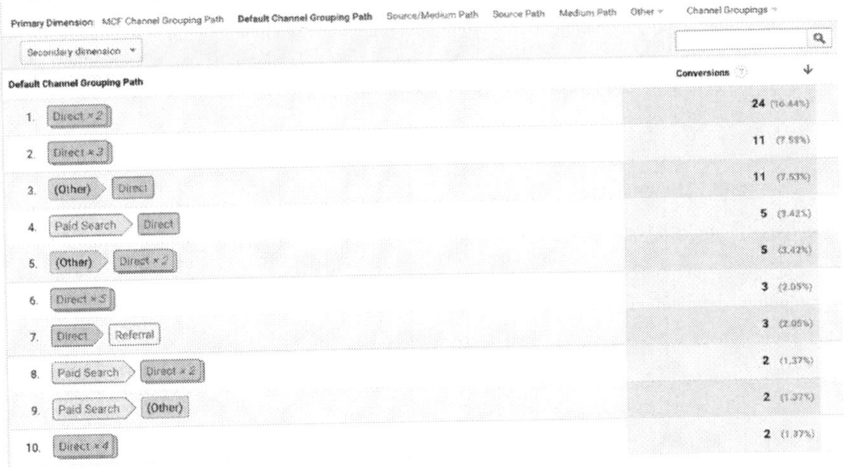

CONVERSION ATTRIBUTION TO FIRST OR LAST CLICK

Most of the time, we only value the last click or the last channel, when in fact, there may have been more than 5 touch points on their conversion path.

So, an interesting report is to see to whom we assign the value of the conversion: to the first click that led the way to the conversion? the last click that finally pulled it off, or a combination of both? This is what you can analyse through the 'Attribution'> Model comparison tool.

For example, if we only look at Google Analytics or the Search Console, we might discover that most of the traffic on our website comes from people searching for the brand name; but, these users searched generically on Google for a product. They probably clicked on one of your ads, then your remarketing campaigns showed a banner on some website, they saw your post on Facebook, and finally, they googled your brand, clicked and bought through the first organic result.

Given this example, we cannot think that it was only the SEO result that was successful and that the money invested in social, display and paid search were useless. Our attribution model has to give credit and even return of investment to all these channels and paid campaigns.

In this section, you will see how many conversions or income came if the attribution is switched from the last click to the first or another such as linear, giving equal value to all touch points.

CUSTOM REPORTS ON GOOGLE ANALYTICS

From the moment you access the Analytics home page, you will find the top values in a given time range, which you can change in the upper right corner. You can also configure your own reports using different charts, tables, and maps.

Just click on 'Customization' / 'Dashboards' and '+Create' to create a new visualization of your information. On the right-hand side, you will see a suggestion for you to browse their gallery where others have already created their reports, and you can easily import them. You can also access from here: https://www.google.com/analytics/gallery/

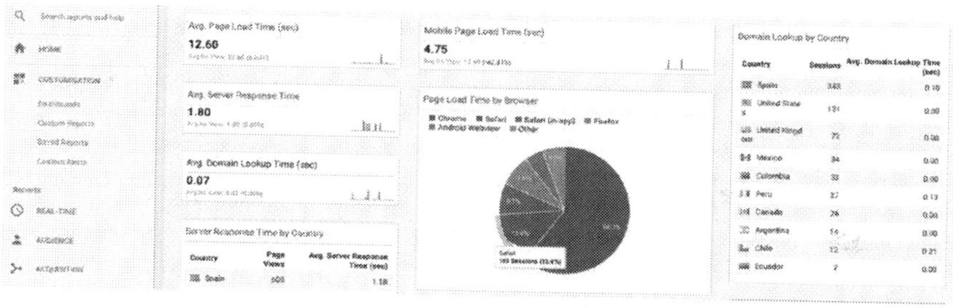

38. GOOGLE SEARCH CONSOLE

YOUR WEBSITE'S PERFORMANCE

Formerly known as Google Webmaster Tool, the Google Search Console will help you to properly configure your website for Google bots to scan and track your web performance.

By validating your web property in this tool, you will get several information about your organic ranking, which you can not get through Google Analytics alone, such as in what organic position your web appeared for a certain query.

In addition, it will allow you to diagnose the main problems that could impact the rankings that we already saw in Step 2, such as blocking robots through your robots.txt file, the number of pages indexed that Google has tracked through your sitemap.xml, the time it takes the web to load, among other features.

KEY USES OF GOOGLE SEARCH CONSOLE

Before going into details about its configuration (which is very simple), I prefer to comment on the value you will get by using this tool:

- You are going to make sure that Google can access and track your site and show it in its organic results.
- Inform Google about the new content on your website, so it can track and rank it as soon as possible, as well as deleting results that you do not want to be displaying anymore.
- Monitor the positioning of your website for certain searches, and see how your visibility increases week by week by checking the number of impressions. Remember that Google Analytics shows you the traffic to your website, but here you find out how many times you appeared in Google despite not getting the click.

- Structure your content, which can be very useful if you have an online store since you show Google where the price is, title, product SKU, and other things are and analyse all similar pages with the same structure.
- Mobile performance.
- Which websites have links to your page as we covered in Step 2 - link building.

CONFIGURE YOUR WEBSITE IN GOOGLE SEARCH CONSOLE

To set up your website in Google Search Console, access google.com/webmasters/ with the Gmail address you use in all your Google services and log in with the button on the right. Once inside, click the tab on the right that says 'add site' and enter the URL.

You will have several options to verify that you are the owner of the website like inserting some type of code or uploading a file so it means have access to the folders.

Another very quick way is through Google Analytics since in order to add that property, you already had to add your piece of code on the header. Or you can download a small HTML file which you will have to upload to the root of your web folder via FTP connection. When you have uploaded it, click on 'verify' and Google will access that address to check that you have placed it.

INTEGRATION OF GOOGLE ANALYTICS WITH SEARCH CONSOLE

The good thing about all these Google products is that they can be interlaced and exposed to the maximum, as is the case of Analytics with AdWords, AdSense and Search Console.

The three tools are independent and inform you of different things; so by linking them all, you will pass the information from one another, and you will get to see a holistic picture and much more information on each one of them.

To link the properties, go to the configuration of your website in Google Search Console with the button at your right and select 'Google Analytics Property'. It will show you a list of the different properties that you have in Google Analytics. Select it and save it.

IDENTIFY AND FIX TRACKING ISSUES

In the menu on the left, you will identify a very important section called 'Crawl'. Here you will find different sub-sections, such as 'Crawl Errors', which informs you of all the anomalies that Google has encountered when scanning the site and all the response codes it obtained which could be affecting users' experience, such as Internal Server Error 500, or pages not found as 404 errors.

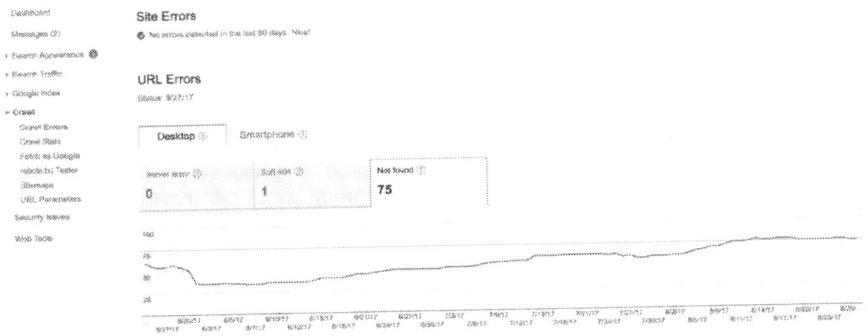

In 'Crawl stats', you can also detect an unexpected increase of time downloading a page. Perhaps the last video you uploaded is difficult for browsers to handle, which you should change or optimise.

The 'robots.txt tester' warns you of possible bad settings and blocks for Google crawling your site. Apart from showing you the lines of code creating the conflict if any, it allows you to verify that everything is scanned correctly by entering one of the pages of your website (or the main URL), and click on test.

Another key file in providing an easy reading to robots is the sitemap.xml file. In its subsection, it informs you about possible incidences in the reading of certain pages. I recommend that you check their status since even if you see only warnings and not errors, their recidivism could result in errors.

ANALYZE YOUR SEO RANKING

In the 'Search Appearance' section, you will find the following information, which can help you to optimise your site better towards specific keywords:

Search Analysis

As I said at the beginning of this chapter, the advantage of using the Search Console was because of the information that we cannot obtain from other tools like Analytics, since here, we observe not only the traffic our website receives but also the times that our site appeared in Google' search results for certain searches (Impressions) and the average position it appeared.

It's very easy to see the difference of clicks and CTRs your result gets due to being at a higher or lower position. You will see that sometimes, you appeared in very low positions but for words that were not very relevant or in which you do not even want to be ranked for, so it is important to group these results into what you really want to appear and optimise for and ignore the others.

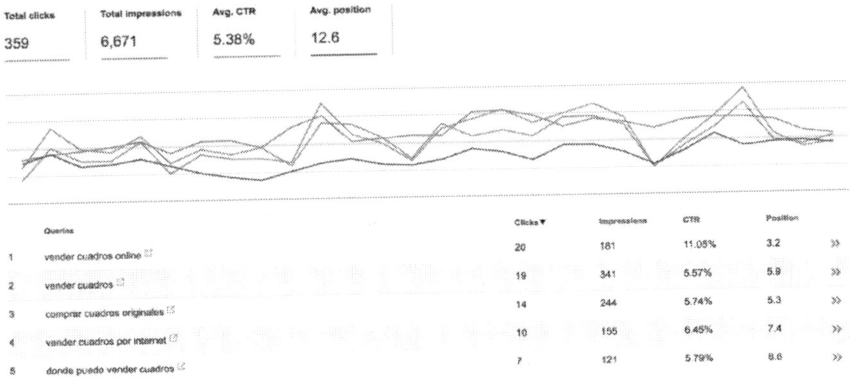

Links to your site

In this section, you will discover which websites are sending users to your site from theirs, and what is the phrase they linked to your domain. Most will link the word of your brand, but it can sometimes be a group of words, like 'The best hotel on the south coast'. So, it is easier for Google to know why you are being linked more than if it was only the word 'here', from 'click <u>here</u> to find out more'.

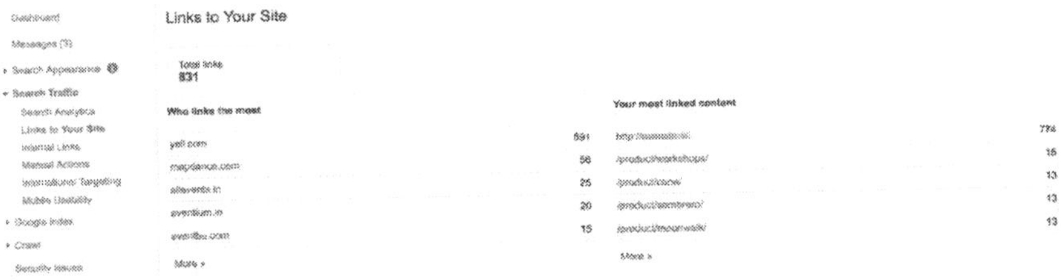

39. GOOGLE ADSENSE: MONETISATION REPORT

The AdSense tool is far away from being at the same level of AdWords' development. The main reason is that the latter is the one that generates money to Google, and the former is where Google pays to website's owners. Therefore, optimization functions or reports leaves much to be desired; but hey, at least it gives us some basic information about which ads or ad placements on your web generates more income.

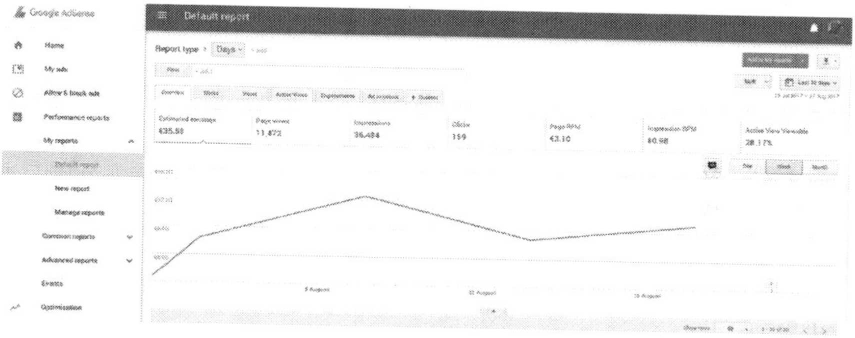

You can identify which ads have worked best and find patterns on their characteristics that allow you to make decisions to get an income increase each month.

Detect elements to optimise your site based on the data you have:

Which ad size works best? Of the ones you have placed on your website, maybe some work better than others. For example, the bigger they are, the more clicks they generate. This may also be conditioned by others of the following characteristics, so you should try to make a fair comparison.

Text, Images or Rich Media? In general, dynamic ads (Rich Media) are more eye-catching and perform better. Although in my experience, text ads work very well if you combine them with the content of your website since users may think that they are better integrated and less intrusive, and the text also offers more lines of content and information about what the user can expect from the destination URL.

Ad position. The dilemma of wanting to hide ads down the page goes against trying to get more income by placing them in the header. Google will pay more for the clicks you generate from the ads shown right away when the user lands on, which means, the ones as high as possible. It is even more important when the visits come from mobile devices.

If your web generates a lot of traffic, I would advise you to even monetise the web for impressions, rather than clicks. Or that could be something else to test!

40. GOOGLE DATA STUDIO: REPORT OF REPORTS

Google has launched a new tool which you can access from Google Analytics by clicking on its matrix icon on the upper right corner (or directly through datastudio.google.com).

Google Data Studio allows you to create a visual report in a complete and simple way by importing directly and effortlessly all the information from other Google properties, like Google Analytics, AdWords, YouTube, Google Docs, among others.

You can start from templates or create reports from scratch by controlling, not only all the information displayed but also its design, distribution, images, and text; achieving a completely professional finish which you can share through a link.

Because they are online and live (based on Google Docs or Drive), you can view the updated information whenever you access the report, and you can dynamically change the dates of the data shown, as you would on the individual platforms.

The good thing about using this report viewer is that you will be able to group different information that are related to one another. This allows you to have a more holistic view of what's happening on all your websites and online channels, such as detailing the keywords and costs of your Advertising campaigns, while Google Analytics information will add to the mix the behaviour of users on your specific pages.

The visualization of graphs, numbers, comparatives or tables, are very versatile and intuitive. You only have to imagine what you would like to represent, and play a bit with editing the data, with its rows and columns, until you get what you want. Anyway, it is always better to start with a predesigned template and edit it to learn how the tool works internally.

At the moment, the tool does not yet integrate with other non-Google platforms like Facebook or Twitter, but I imagine it is on its roadmap, and maybe when you read this book, it has already evolved more.

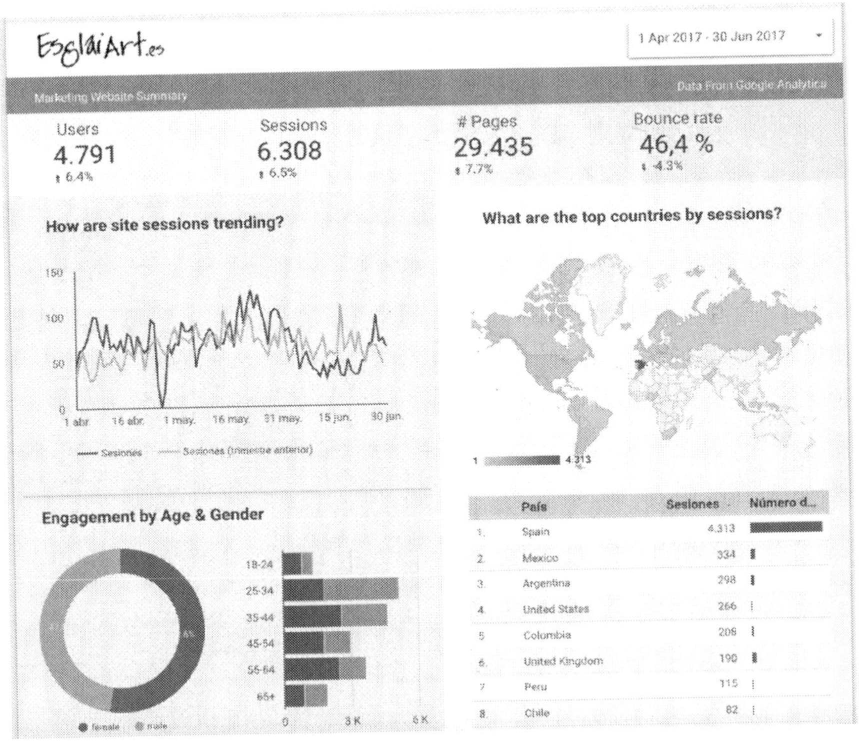

41. SUPERMETRICS FOR MULTIPLE DATA SOURCES

YOUR ONLINE REPORT INTEGRATING WITH GOOGLE DOCS AND DATASTUDIO

This extension for Google Docs has similar functions to those described in Google Data Studio, but it integrates more channels that are not from Google (e.g. Facebook ads, LinkedIn ads or Twitter ads) and displays all data as tables in Google Spreadsheets or to pass the data directly to your Data Studio report.

Supermetrics prevent you from having to go to all these channels separately every day or every week to see what happened with your KPIs. In one click, you will have a complete report of all your websites and all your channels (like AdWords, Search Console, Analytics, Facebook, Bing, etc.) importing all your information for different periods of time and with the filters you want applied.

To add this extension to Google Docs, just google 'supermetrics google extension' and click on the first link from chrome.google.com. You will install it by clicking on 'free' and it will direct you to Google Sheets. You will have to grant some of the accesses they request.

A sidebar will open on the right, but if you do not find it, you can also load it by going to the top menu: Add-ons> Supermetrics> Launch sidebar.

Configure the channels that you want to import data from and manage your metrics as a table, bar graph, circular or linear. The channels you can import data from are:

- Bing ads: Bing advertising information.
- LinkedIn ads: Data from your professional B2B paid campaigns.
- Facebook ads: Information about your social ad campaigns.

- Facebook Insights: If you are a multipage Facebook administrator, you could see: from each page: its new fans, or the opposite, people who have stopped following you, its organic reach of your publications (free posts) or through a paid campaign, the number of comments, likes, among others.
- Google AdWords: Your advertising information on Google campaigns.
- Google Analytics: allows you to bring all the information that is also accessible from Analytics, but with the added value that here you can filter all the metrics related to other channels and get a complete picture of everything that can have an impact when trying to get more customers or visitors. For example, if one day, you have a peak of visits to your website after a Facebook post, you can see with Supermetrics, how many new fans you got or lost that day.
- Google Search Console: you can use it to import information about the organic ranking of your pages, keywords that bring traffic, pages or indexed images, etc.

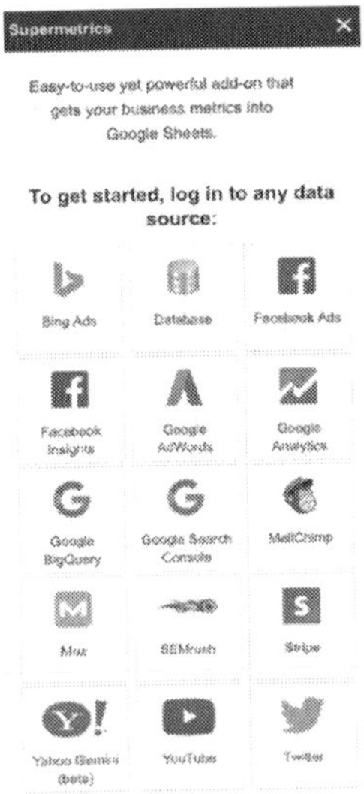

I use it a lot to keep track of all the traffic on my websites. I create an individual tab per web or client in which I analyse their site in much detail to offer complete reports and not only visits, adding YouTube views, new or lost 'likes', website performance on mobile devices, among many other things, which allows us to see the impact of a campaign in a 360° view. This software allows us to see the holistic image of all our online activity and the interconnections between media.

42. HOOTSUITE FOR YOUR SOCIAL NETWORKS

MONITOR WHAT PEOPLE ARE SAYING

This section doesn't refer to paid or promoted publications, like I said on Step 4 about Facebook, Instagram, and other paid social networks, but about the free and organic posts we are all used to creating in our personal life.

Now, we want to give that human face to our brand through good digital content management, and to start building (or maintaining if you already have it) a good network of contacts, followers, and fans that will spread the word to their friends.

Hootsuite is one of the most used, easy, and free tool to manage all your company's or website's profiles and pages on social networks, apart from also being able to monitor and listen to everything that is said about you in those networks, about your business, or related to any keyword you think is relevant.

It is designed for companies of every size and any number of followers you have on Facebook or Twitter. So, if you have a medium or large company and you have delegated all your social publications to an employee of an external agency, you can do it without fear through the different levels of access offered in Hootsuite, and with high-security standards.

You do not want a wrong comment to be seen by thousands of fans in the name of your company. That would not be the first time that happens, so you have to be very careful on who gets access since what happens online, stays forever in one way or another.

The voice and opinion of your users (or yourself as a consumer) has more weight than ever, and the conversation between them and your company is more direct and accessible than it has ever been before. You will know it from your experience as a user when you sent a direct message through Facebook to a very large company without awaiting an answer, and suddenly the answered in less than two hours, that's the new and awesome customer service. Or when you have complained, named and tagged a company, and the company has replied on the same public conversation in the most correct and positive way to change your negative sentiment and those from all the people you influenced.

There are other companies that still decide to ignore what is said on social networks, thinking that it will not impact them, but they are making a serious mistake. Today, every opinion on social networks matters and you need to look after your company's ones.

CUSTOMISE YOUR SOCIAL DASHBOARD

Once you have created a free account in hootsuite.com, you will access a dashboard where you will add different columns within a specific tab, so it is up to you to decide how you want to organise this social structure.

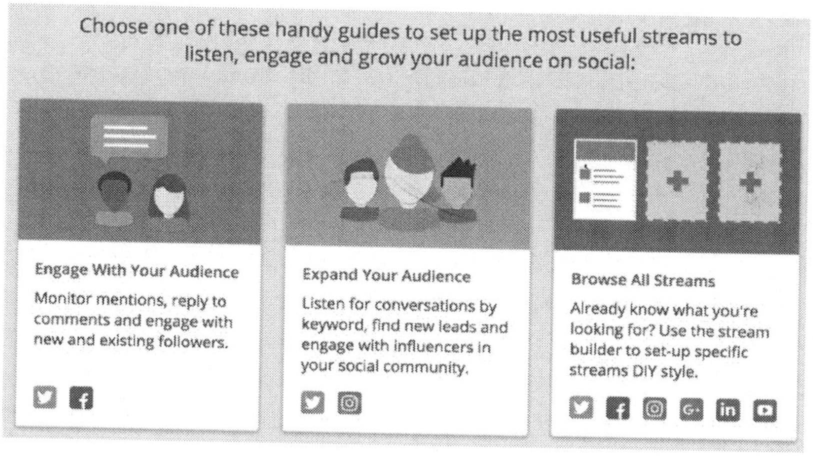

I personally like to have 3 tabs. In one, I have all my publications or company profiles; in another, I monitor what interests me across the network, and in the third tab, I identify profiles of potential competitors to monitor what they do on their social networks. Another very common way of organizing would be to create a tab per social network and visualise everything about that network on the screen. If you have several businesses, you could have them grouped with that logic.

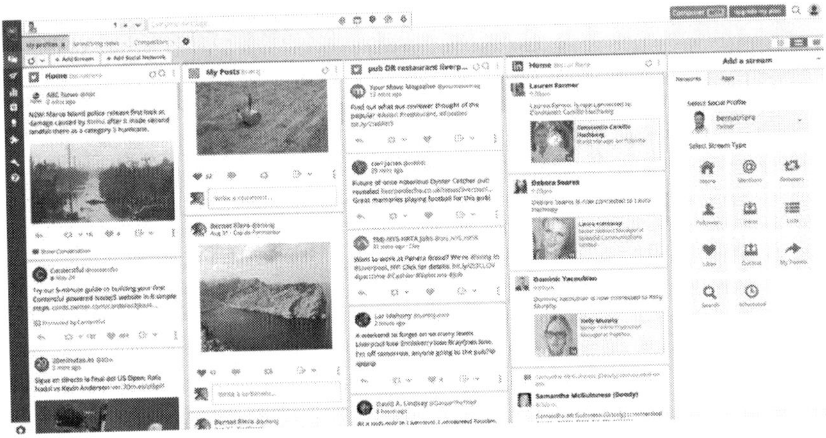

At the top, you will see a bar where you can create messages and distribute them at the same time through different profiles, reducing your workload.

In addition, you can schedule them for a future time, which would allow you, for example, to write all your tweets on a Sunday night in 30 minutes and then publish them throughout the week, so you can forget about that for a while.

As you see, in the first tab of my dashboard that I designed for this example, I'm showing my Twitter newsfeed, my Instagram publications, Twitter searches about 'pubs or restaurants in Liverpool', which will be updated every time someone tweets about these keywords, and finally the newsfeed from my professional network LinkedIn, among many other possibilities.

The columns will be determined by the information of each specific social network, which can be: Facebook, Twitter, Instagram, Google+, LinkedIn, WordPress and YouTube.

THANK YOU

This is my first self-published book and I'm trying to prove my point of being able to rank at the top on search engines like Amazon as well as generating small, passive royalties as I suggested in the first chapter.

I hope I gave you some value for your career or business. The best feedback I can get would be a review from your Amazon account so that you're helping other entrepreneurs with similar needs to find this book.

If you have built an online business that is generating passive income, or you have managed to create fantastic new opportunities for your business which is visible online, please also share these stories with me. I'd love to hear them! Email me: info@bernatriera.es

60483616R00151

Made in the USA
San Bernardino, CA
11 December 2017